AF322575

Empire's Aftershocks:
The Enduring Impact of British Colonial Policy

Nigel Pickerton

Title: Empire's Aftershocks: The Enduring Impact of British Colonial Policy
Author: Nigel Pickerton

Published by Taida Publishing
taidapublishing.com

This book is a work of nonfiction. The events and facts depicted are based on thorough research. Every effort has been made to ensure accuracy in the details of historical events and sources. However, interpretations of historical facts are the author's own and do not necessarily reflect the views of any organization, institution, or publisher.

The publisher and the author disclaim any liability for any errors or omissions or for any damages resulting from the use or interpretation of the material contained in this book.

ISBN: 979-8-89214-111-6
Cover Illustration: Hubert Anker

First Edition

Table of Contents

INTRODUCTION

The overarching impact of the British Empire's catastrophic decisions has left an indelible mark on the modern world. The lines drawn on maps, the policies implemented, and the social structures imposed by British colonial rule continue to shape the geopolitical landscape, fueling ongoing tensions and conflicts.

The partition of India in 1947 is a prime example of how British decisions have sown seeds of lasting turmoil. The hurried and poorly planned division created India and Pakistan, with the contentious region of Kashmir becoming a flash point for conflict. The subsequent wars, communal violence, and displacement of millions have their roots in the arbitrary borders drawn by British colonial authorities. The creation of Bangladesh in 1971, after a brutal conflict, further exemplifies the long-term consequences of these divisions.

Similarly, British policies in the Middle East, such as the Sykes-Picot Agreement and the Balfour Declaration, have left a legacy of conflict and instability. The artificial borders created by the Sykes-Picot Agreement ignored the complex ethnic, religious, and cultural realities of the region, leading to long-standing disputes and rivalries. The Balfour Declaration set the stage for the Israeli-Arab conflict, a source of profound and unrelenting violence and tension in the Middle East.

In Africa, the legacy of the Scramble for Africa and the arbitrary borders drawn by colonial powers have resulted in numerous conflicts and civil wars. The imposition of indirect rule and the entrenchment of ethnic divisions have contributed to political instability and violence in countries such as Nigeria, Sudan, and Rwanda. The Mau Mau Uprising in Kenya and the brutal suppression that followed highlight the deep scars left by British colonial policies.

These historical decisions are not just relics of the past but are central to understanding many of today's conflicts. The modern world needs to move beyond the decisions and lines on a map made by colonial powers. Addressing these legacies requires a concerted effort to promote reconciliation, justice, and equitable development. It involves recognizing historical injustices and developing resolutions that uphold the dignity and aspirations of all impacted groups.

The British policies covered in this book are a significant cause of today's conflicts. By understanding the roots of these issues, we can better address their consequences and work toward a more peaceful and just world. The process of decolonization is ongoing, and it requires a commitment to healing historical wounds and fostering global cooperation. Only by confronting the past can we hope to build a future free from the shadows of colonialism, where the lines drawn by imperial powers no longer dictate the lives and destinies of millions.

Overview of the British Empire's global reach and influence

In history, few entities have exerted as profound an influence on the world stage as the British Empire. At its zenith, it was an unparalleled colossus, a vast, sprawling network of territories that spanned continents and oceans, indelibly shaping the modern era's political, economic, and cultural landscapes. This chapter explores the British Empire's global reach and influence, unraveling the complexities of its expansion, administration, and lasting legacy.

The genesis and expansion of the empire

The roots of the British Empire can be traced back to the late sixteenth century, a period characterized by intense maritime exploration and burgeoning commercial interests. In 1588, the collapse of the Spanish Armada marked the dawn of England's naval supremacy, a critical factor in its imperial ambitions. The subsequent establishment of the East India Company in 1600 signaled the beginning of a strategic and sustained effort to dominate overseas trade and acquire territorial footholds.

The seventeenth and eighteenth centuries witnessed the Empire's rapid expansion. The formation of colonies across North America, the Caribbean, and India set the stage for a global network that would eventually encompass nearly a quarter of the world's landmass and population. By the nineteenth century, British control had extended to Africa, Southeast Asia, and the Pacific, transforming the empire into the largest and most powerful in history. This expansion was not only territorial but also ideological, driven by a complex interplay of economic aspirations, strategic considerations, and a sense of civilizational mission.

Administrative strategies and governance

The British Empire's administrative framework was a mosaic of diverse governance models, each tailored to the unique circumstances of the respective colonies. Local self-governance was gradually introduced in settler colonies like Canada and Australia, fostering a sense of political autonomy within the imperial structure. In contrast, in regions such as India and Africa, the British employed a combination of direct and indirect rule, leveraging existing power structures and local elites to maintain control.

The principle of indirect rule, famously articulated by Lord Lugard, was influential in Africa. This approach allowed the British to administer vast territories with minimal expenditure and personnel by co-opting traditional leaders and integrating Indigenous institutions into the colonial administration. However, this strategy also entrenched existing hierarchies and sowed the seeds of future ethnic and political conflicts.

The Indian subcontinent, often regarded as the jewel in the crown of the British Empire, exemplifies the complexities of British colonial governance. The East India Company's initial foothold in the early seventeenth century evolved into direct Crown rule following the Indian Rebellion of 1857. The establishment of the British Raj marked a period of extensive administrative reforms, infrastructural development, and economic exploitation. The introduction of the railways, telegraph, and modern education systems were touted as progressive contributions, yet they were primarily designed to serve British economic and strategic interests.

Economic exploitation and global trade networks

The economic motivations underpinning the British Empire's expansion cannot be overstated. The pursuit of wealth through the control of resources, markets, and trade routes was a driving force behind colonial policies. The mercantilist economic doctrine of the seventeenth and eighteenth centuries emphasized the accumulation of wealth through a favorable balance of trade, leading to the establishment of monopolistic trading companies like the East India Company and the Hudson's Bay Company.

The Industrial Revolution in Britain catalyzed a shift toward a more integrated global economy, with the colonies serving as both suppliers of raw materials and markets for manufactured goods. The exploitation of India's cotton and opium, the Caribbean's sugar, and Africa's minerals and rubber underscored the extractive nature of colonial economies. These economic activities generated immense wealth for Britain, fueling its industrial growth and global dominance while simultaneously impoverishing and destabilizing the colonized regions.

Cultural hegemony and the Mission Civilisatrice

Beyond the tangible economic and political dimensions, the British Empire exerted a profound cultural influence on its colonies. The dissemination of the English language, legal systems, educational frameworks, and social norms facilitated a form of cultural hegemony that endured long after formal colonial rule. The British presented their imperial mission as a civilizing endeavor, a paternalistic responsibility to uplift and modernize the "uncivilized" peoples of the world.

This civilizing mission, however, was fraught with contradictions and hypocrisies. While the British touted the virtues of liberty, justice, and progress, their colonial practices often entailed brutal repression, racial discrimination, and economic exploitation. The imposition of Western cultural norms frequently resulted in the gradual decline of Indigenous traditions and identities, creating a complex legacy of cultural hybridity and resistance.

Legacy and global impact

The profound and often paradoxical consequences of the British Empire have shaped the modern world uniquely. On the one hand, the empire's contributions to global connectivity, technological advancement, and institutional frameworks are undeniable. The spread of the English language, common law, parliamentary democracy, and international trade networks can be traced back to the colonial era.

On the other hand, the scars of colonialism are starkly visible in the form of enduring economic disparities, geopolitical tensions, and social inequalities. The arbitrary borders drawn by colonial administrators have fueled conflicts in regions including the Middle East, Africa, and South Asia. The economic structures established during colonial rule have left a legacy of dependency and underdevelopment in many former colonies.

In conclusion, the British Empire's global reach and influence were characterized by a complex interplay of power, exploitation, and cultural exchange. Its legacy continues to shape the contemporary world's political, economic, and cultural landscapes, necessitating a nuanced and rigorous examination of its history.

Explanation of "catastrophic decisions" and their long-term impacts

History is replete with decisions that, at first glance, seemed poised to yield progress and prosperity, only to unravel as catastrophic misjudgments with repercussions that reverberated through generations. In the context of the British Empire, such decisions were not just miscalculations, but deliberate policies and actions taken with a blend of hubris and a severe underestimation of their far-reaching consequences.

The concept of catastrophic decisions in this discourse refers to those pivotal moments and policies that, rather than cementing British imperial dominance and benevolence, have fueled ongoing discord, conflict, and strife. These decisions often emerged from a complex matrix of economic ambitions, strategic necessities, and a paternalistic mindset that assumed an inherent superiority of British civilization over the diverse cultures it sought to dominate.

Consider, for instance, the Sykes-Picot Agreement of 1916, a clandestine arrangement between Britain and France to partition the Ottoman Empire's territories in the Middle East. This agreement divided the region into artificial states with little regard for ethnic, religious, and historical continuity due to strategic considerations and the demands of wartime diplomacy. The immediate consequence was a fragile peace, but the long-term impact has been an almost perpetual state of conflict and instability that persists to this day. Such a decision, catastrophic in its disregard for the complexities of local identities, underscores the pernicious legacy of imperial arrogance.

Similarly, the Partition of India in 1947 stands as a stark illustration of how a hasty and ill-conceived decision can lead to a humanitarian disaster. One of the largest mass migrations in history and communal violence that claimed hundreds of thousands of lives were the results of Cyril Radcliffe's hasty border demarcation, a British lawyer who was unfamiliar with the intricacies of the subcontinent. The legacy of this partition is etched into the psyches of India and Pakistan, manifesting in recurrent tensions and conflicts over Kashmir, a region left disputed by the arbiters of the partition.

These examples, among many others, form the crux of our exploration into the British Empire's catastrophic decisions. Each chapter will dissect a specific policy or event, tracing its origins, motivations, and immediate outcomes. More importantly, we will explore the long-term consequences of these decisions, unraveling how they have shaped contemporary geopolitical landscapes, social structures, and cultural identities.

Brief overview of the book's structure and objectives

This book is meticulously structured to offer a comprehensive yet accessible examination of the British Empire's most consequential decisions and their long-term effects. It is divided into thematic sections, each focusing on a specific geographical region or a notable facet of imperial policy. This organization not only facilitates a coherent narrative flow but also allows for a detailed, region-specific analysis.

"Part 1: Catastrophic Decisions and Their Global Impact" sets the stage by examining pivotal moments with wide-ranging consequences. This section provides a macro-level overview, establishing the foundational themes that will be explored in greater depth in subsequent parts.

"Part 2: Regional Case Studies" delves into the specific experiences of different regions under British rule. Each chapter is dedicated to a distinct region—such as the Middle East, the Indian Subcontinent, and Africa—unpacking the unique ways in which British decisions manifested and their particular long-term impacts.

"Part 3: Southeast Asia and the Pacific" examines British policies and their repercussions in Southeast Asia and Oceania. This part highlights the complex interactions between imperial strategies and local societies, illuminating the lasting consequences of these encounters.

"Part 4: The Caribbean and Ireland" explores the British Empire's influence in the Caribbean and Ireland, focusing on the legacy of slavery, colonial governance, and the struggles for independence.

"Part 5: Thematic Analyses" shifts the focus to overarching themes such as economic exploitation, cultural policies, and administrative strategies. By examining these themes across different regions, this section aims to highlight the common patterns and systemic issues inherent in British imperial policies.

"Part 6: Legal and Administrative Legacies" addresses the introduction of British legal systems and administrative policies, their conflicts with local traditions, and their influence on contemporary governance structures.

"Part 7: Resistance, Rebellion, and Postcolonial Challenges" examines the myriad ways in which colonized people resisted British rule and the subsequent challenges they faced in the postcolonial era. This part brings to the forefront the colonized communities' initiative, presenting a nuanced exploration of insurgency dynamics and the intricate aftermath of colonial governance.

"Part 8: Interdisciplinary and Comparative Perspectives" integrates insights from various disciplines—history, sociology, economics, and political science—to provide a multifaceted analysis of the long-term impacts of British imperialism. This section also includes comparative studies with other colonial empires, offering a broader context for understanding the British Empire's unique characteristics and lasting influences.

"Part 9: Environmental Impacts: Environmental Degradation." The focus on resource extraction and the introduction of non-native species had substantial impacts on the environments of many colonies. Issues such as deforestation, loss of biodiversity, and soil degradation are among the long-lasting environmental consequences that continue to affect former colonies.

"Part 10: Social and Human Rights Issues: Human Rights Abuses." The British Empire's history includes numerous human rights abuses, such as forced labor, land dispossession, and violent repression of resistance movements. These actions left deep scars and continue to influence the pursuit of justice and reconciliation in former colonies.

The objectives of this book are manifold. First, it aims to provide a thorough and detailed analysis of the British Empire's most significant decisions, revealing the intricate web of causes and consequences that define these historical moments. Second, it seeks to foster a more in-depth understanding of how these decisions continue to shape contemporary global issues, from geopolitical conflicts to socioeconomic disparities. Finally, it aspires to contribute to the ongoing discourse on imperialism, decolonization, and historical justice, encouraging readers to reflect on the lessons of the past and their relevance to the present and future.

Combining rigorous scholarship with an engaging narrative, this book serves as both an educational resource and a compelling reading experience. By weaving granular detail with broader analytical insights, it seeks to bring the complexities of the British Empire's legacy into sharp focus, inviting readers to engage with history in an intellectually enriching and highly resonant way.

By examining these themes, the book aims to provide a comprehensive understanding of how the British Empire's catastrophic decisions have shaped the modern world. It emphasizes the interconnectedness of these impacts and the importance of addressing them to build a more just and fair future.

PROLOGUE

The British Empire: a brief history

The British Empire, often hailed as the most extensive empire in history, epitomized the zenith of British global influence and dominance. Its roots lie deep in the sixteenth century, a time when maritime exploration and trade became the lifeblood of burgeoning European powers. What began as a series of tentative voyages across uncharted seas evolved into a formidable imperial enterprise that spanned the globe by the early twentieth century.

Early beginnings: the age of exploration

The genesis of the British Empire can be traced back to the rule of Queen Elizabeth I in 1588. The defeat of the Spanish Armada that same year heralded a new era of naval supremacy for England, enabling the nation to assert its influence over the seas. Due to the allure of new trade routes and territories, pioneering explorers like Sir Francis Drake and Sir Walter Raleigh ventured into the unknown. These early forays laid the groundwork for the establishment of overseas colonies and trading posts.

The foundation of the East India Company in 1600 marked a pivotal moment in British imperial history. This joint-stock company, granted a royal charter by Elizabeth I, was vested with the authority to wage war, negotiate treaties, and establish settlements in pursuit of trade. Over time, it would transform from a commercial entity into a powerful political force, underpinning British dominance in the Indian subcontinent.

Expansion and consolidation: the seventeenth and eighteenth centuries

The seventeenth century witnessed the expansion of British influence in the Americas, with the establishment of colonial outposts in New England, Virginia, and the Caribbean. The cultivation of profitable cash crops such as tobacco and sugar, supported by the harsh system of transatlantic slavery, generated immense wealth for Britain. The Navigation Acts of the mid-seventeenth century further cemented British mercantile interests by ensuring that colonial trade benefited the mother country.

The eighteenth century saw the consolidation of British power in India, a process marked by a series of military victories and strategic alliances. The Battle of Plassey in 1757 and the subsequent Battle of Buxar in 1764 solidified the East India Company's control over Bengal, a region rich in resources and economic potential. These victories were not just military triumphs but signified the emergence of Britain as a dominant imperial power in Asia.

The Seven Years' War (1756–1763), often described as the first global conflict, further extended British influence. The Treaty of Paris (1763) ceded significant French territories in North America and the Caribbean to Britain, reaffirming its status as the preeminent colonial power. However, the American Revolution (1775–1783) dealt a severe blow to British imperial ambitions, resulting in the loss of the thirteen American colonies. Despite this setback, the British Empire continued to expand, turning its gaze toward new opportunities in Africa, Asia, and the Pacific.

The apex of empire: the nineteenth and early twentieth centuries

The nineteenth century was characterized by an unprecedented expansion of British imperial influence, often referred to as the "Age of Imperialism." The Industrial Revolution provided the technological and economic impetus for this expansion, enabling Britain to project its global power with unmatched efficiency. Railways, steamships, and telegraphs revolutionized transportation and communication, knitting the vast empire together into a cohesive whole.

In India, the dissolution of the East India Company following the Indian Rebellion of 1857 led to the establishment of direct Crown rule, marking the beginning of the British Raj. This period saw significant infrastructural development, including the construction of extensive railway networks and irrigation systems. However, these developments primarily served British economic interests and often exacerbated social and economic inequalities.

The Berlin Conference of 1884–1885 epitomized the "Scramble for Africa," during which European powers, led by Britain and France, partitioned the African continent with little regard for Indigenous cultures and societies. By the turn of the century, Britain had established control over vast swathes of Africa, from Egypt in the north to South Africa in the south. This period also saw the annexation of territories in Southeast Asia and the Pacific, further extending the empire's global reach.

Strategic imperatives and ideological motivations

A complex interplay of strategic imperatives and ideological motivations drove the expansion of the British Empire. The desire to control key trade routes and resources, coupled with the need to secure naval bases and coaling stations, underpinned many imperial ventures. The 1869 completion of the Suez Canal, for instance, significantly shortened the sea route to India and became a vital artery of the British Empire.

Ideologically, the British Empire was justified through a paternalistic belief in the civilizing mission. Proponents of imperialism argued that Britain had a moral duty to spread Christianity, Western education, and modern governance to the "backward" people of the world. This notion of the white man's burden, popularized by Rudyard Kipling, provided a veneer of benevolence to what was, in essence, a project of economic exploitation and political dominance.

Decline and legacy

The two World Wars of the twentieth century marked the beginning of the end for the British Empire. The economic strain of war, coupled with the rise of nationalist movements in the colonies, eroded British control. The Indian independence movement, spearheaded by figures like Mahatma Gandhi and Jawaharlal Nehru, culminated in the 1947 partition, which resulted in the division and emergence of India and Pakistan. This event signaled the unraveling of British imperial power in Asia.

The postwar period witnessed a wave of decolonization across Africa and the Caribbean as newly independent nations moved beyond the shadow of colonial rule. The Suez Crisis of 1956, during which Britain was forced to withdraw from Egypt under international pressure, underscored the decline of British influence on the global stage.

Today, the legacy of the British Empire is a complex and contentious subject. On one hand, it contributed to the spread of the English language, legal systems, and democratic institutions. On the other hand, it left a legacy of economic exploitation, cultural disruption, and political instability. The arbitrary borders drawn by colonial administrators continue to fuel conflicts in regions such as the Middle East, Africa, and South Asia.

In conclusion, the British Empire's global reach and influence were characterized by ambition, ingenuity, and ruthlessness. Its impact on the world, both positive and negative, is still felt today, necessitating a nuanced and critical examination of its history.

Part I

Catastrophic Decisions and Their Global Impact

CHAPTER 1
THE SYKES-PICOT AGREEMENT

The Sykes-Picot Agreement, negotiated in secret during World War I and revealed to the public in 1916, is often cited as one of the most significant and ill-fated decisions in the history of the British Empire. Named after its architects, Sir Mark Sykes of Britain and François Georges-Picot of France, the agreement aimed to define their intended domains of authority and governance in the Middle East after the anticipated defeat of the Ottoman Empire.

The motivations behind the agreement were manifold. For Britain, securing control over regions such as Mesopotamia (modern-day Iraq) was driven by strategic interests, including protecting routes to India, and controlling vital oil resources. In comparison, France was interested in consolidating its influence in Syria and Lebanon, regions historically linked to French cultural and religious missions.

The agreement carved the Ottoman Empire's territories into artificial borders with scant regard for the ethnic, religious, and cultural complexities of the region. Britain was to control areas including Baghdad and Basra, while France would dominate the coastal lands of Syria and Lebanon. Palestine was designated for international administration, reflecting the conflicting interests in the area.

The immediate consequence of the Sykes-Picot Agreement was the fostering of deep-seated resentment and mistrust among the Arab populations, who had been promised independence by the British in exchange for their support against the Ottomans. The revelation of the agreement by the Bolsheviks in 1917, who had gained access to Tsarist Russia's secret archives, further exacerbated feelings of betrayal.

Long-term impact on Middle Eastern geopolitics and conflicts

The Sykes-Picot Agreement has had lasting and significant effects. The arbitrary borders drawn by Sykes and Picot laid the groundwork for a century of political instability, sectarian conflict, and authoritarian regimes in the Middle East. These borders ignored the intricate mosaic of ethnic and religious groups, forcing disparate communities into newly created nation-states.

In Iraq, the imposition of a new state structure amalgamating Sunni, Shia, and Kurdish regions led to chronic instability and conflict. The central government, often dominated by one sectarian group, struggled to maintain control over the diverse population, resulting in cycles of rebellion and repression.

Similarly, in Syria, the artificial state boundaries compounded internal divisions, contributing to a fragile political landscape that eventually descended into civil war in the twenty-first century. The legacy of the Sykes-Picot Agreement is evident in the ongoing conflicts and the rise of extremist groups that exploit the region's deep-seated divisions.

The agreement also had significant implications for the broader geopolitical dynamics of the Middle East. The British and French mandates, established under the auspices of the League of Nations, effectively institutionalized colonial control under the guise of international legitimacy. This period of mandated rule further entrenched colonial legacies, including economic exploitation, administrative practices, and social hierarchies, which continue to shape the region's political and economic landscapes.

Comparative analysis with other regional divisions

Comparatively, the Sykes-Picot Agreement shares similarities with other colonial decisions that imposed artificial borders without regard for local contexts. For instance, the Berlin Conference of 1884–1885 partitioned Africa among European powers, leading to similarly arbitrary boundaries that have fueled conflicts in postcolonial Africa.

Both the Sykes-Picot Agreement and the Berlin Conference exemplify the colonial disregard for Indigenous cultures and political structures, prioritizing imperial interests over the well-being and stability of local populations. However, the Sykes-Picot Agreement's impact is uniquely intertwined with the complex religious and ethnic fabric of the Middle East, making its consequences particularly intractable.

CHAPTER 2

THE PARTITION OF INDIA

The division of British India in 1947, spawning the sovereign nations of India and Pakistan, serves as yet another glaring instance of a disastrous policy implemented by the British Empire. The roots of partition lay in the complex interplay of religious, political, and social factors that had been simmering for decades. The British policy of "divide and rule," aimed at maintaining control by deepening Hindu-Muslim divisions, played a significant role in exacerbating communal tensions.

As the independence movement gained momentum, led by Jawaharlal Nehru and Mahatma Gandhi for the Indian National Congress and Muhammad Ali Jinnah for the All-India Muslim League, the prospect of a united, independent India became increasingly untenable. Jinnah's demand for a separate Muslim state, Pakistan, was driven by fears of Muslim marginalization in a Hindu-majority India.

The British decision to hastily withdraw and transfer power was influenced by numerous factors, including the economic devastation caused by World War II and the mounting pressures of the independence movement. The responsibility of drawing the new borders fell to Sir Cyril Radcliffe, a British lawyer who had never been to India and had little understanding of its complex social and cultural landscape.

The Radcliffe Line, hastily drawn over the course of a few weeks, partitioned the provinces of Punjab and Bengal according to religious majorities. This arbitrary division triggered one of the most extensive mass migrations in human history, with an estimated fourteen million people displaced as Hindus, Muslims, and Sikhs fled their homes to seek refuge across the newly drawn borders.

Human and geopolitical consequences

The human cost of partition was staggering. Communal violence erupted on an unprecedented scale, resulting in the deaths of about one to two million people. The trauma of partition left deep scars on the collective consciousness of the subcontinent, shaping the national identities of both India and Pakistan.

Partition has had lasting and far-reaching geopolitical consequences. The dispute over Kashmir, a state with a majority Muslim population ruled by a Hindu Maharaja, became a flash point for conflict between India and Pakistan. The decision of the Maharaja to agree to India led to the first Indo-Pakistani war in 1947–1948, establishing a pattern of hostility and warfare that has persisted for decades.

The legacy of partition also affected the internal politics of both nations. In India, integrating diverse states and the challenge of managing a vast, multicultural democracy have been significant. In Pakistan, the secession of East Pakistan to form Bangladesh in 1971 highlighted the fragility of the state structure established at partition.

Comparative insights from other partitions

The partition of India bears comparison with other colonial powers drawing arbitrary borders, such as the division of Palestine in 1947. In both cases, the colonial powers' withdrawal left behind a legacy of conflict and displacement, underscoring the long-term human and geopolitical costs of such decisions.

In conclusion, the Sykes-Picot Agreement and the partition of India are symbolic of the catastrophic decisions made by the British Empire. These decisions, driven by a combination of strategic interests, economic ambitions, and a disregard for local complexities, have left a lasting legacy of conflict and instability. As we explore these and other decisions in greater depth, it is imperative to understand the broader context and sustained repercussions of British imperial policies.

CHAPTER 3

THE SCRAMBLE FOR AFRICA

The late nineteenth-century Scramble for Africa, which saw a frenetic rush by European powers to colonize the African continent, is yet another chapter in the litany of catastrophic decisions by the British Empire. Initiated by the Berlin Conference of 1884–1885, where European nations convened to carve up Africa with little regard for Indigenous populations, the British played a leading role in this imperialistic land grab.

Strategic and economic interests drove Britain's involvement in Africa. The quest for resources such as gold, diamonds, and rubber, coupled with the desire to establish strategic outposts along key maritime routes, propelled British expansion. The creation of borders during this period was a haphazard process, characterized by arbitrary lines drawn on maps with scant consideration for the region's ethnic and cultural landscapes.

These artificial borders amalgamated diverse and often antagonistic ethnic groups into single colonies while simultaneously splitting homogeneous groups across different colonial administrations. For instance, the division of the Yoruba people between Nigeria and Benin, or the splitting of the Somali people among British Somaliland, Italian Somaliland, and French Somaliland, sowed seeds of discord that would later erupt into conflict.

Long-term effects on political stability and ethnic relations

The long-term effects of these colonial borders have been considerably destabilizing. The imposition of artificial boundaries disrupted existing political and social structures, leading to a legacy of conflict and instability. In Nigeria, the British amalgamation of the largely Muslim north with the predominantly Christian and animist south created a divided nation. These divisions have manifested in recurrent ethnic and religious violence, civil war, and political instability.

Similarly, in Rwanda, the colonial manipulation of ethnic identities by both German and Belgian administrators, who categorized the population into Hutu, Tutsi, and Twa based on superficial characteristics and socioeconomic roles, laid the groundwork for the 1994 genocide. While not a British colony, Rwanda's tragic history underscores the broader impact of European colonial practices in Africa.

In Kenya, the Mau Mau Uprising (1952–1960) against British colonial rule was a direct response to land dispossession and social inequalities imposed by colonial policies. The brutal suppression of the uprising, characterized by widespread human rights abuses, left a lasting scar on Kenyan society. The legacy of colonial rule in Kenya is evident in its continued struggles with ethnic tensions and economic disparities.

Comparative analysis with other colonial powers

While the British Empire was not alone in its imperial endeavors in Africa, its approach often stood in stark contrast to that of other colonial powers. French colonial policy, for instance, was characterized by the concept of "assimilation," which aimed to transform colonies into extensions of France through cultural and administrative integration. This policy, however, also resulted in significant resistance and long-term instability in former French colonies.

Particularly in Angola, Mozambique, and the Congo, the Portuguese and Belgian approaches to colonialism were characterized by extreme exploitation and brutality. The lasting impacts of these colonial policies are evident in the persistent conflicts and socioeconomic challenges faced by these nations.

The British policy of indirect rule, particularly articulated by Lord Lugard in Nigeria, aimed to govern through existing local power structures. While this approach minimized administrative costs and initially appeared to maintain stability, it entrenched local hierarchies and exacerbated ethnic divisions, contributing to long-term instability.

Part II

Regional Case Studies

CHAPTER 4

THE MIDDLE EAST

The Balfour Declaration and its impact on Jewish-Arab relations

The Balfour Declaration of 1917, issued by British Foreign Secretary Arthur Balfour, marked another catastrophic decision with long-term consequences. The declaration expressed Britain's support for the establishment of a "national home for the Jewish people" in Palestine, a region then under Ottoman rule and home to a significant Arab population.

The motivations behind the Balfour Declaration were multifaceted. On one level, it was a strategic move to secure Jewish support for the Allied cause during World War I. On the other hand, it was influenced by the Zionist movement's goal of creating a Jewish homeland in Palestine, and by a paternalistic British conviction in their civilizing mission as European colonizers.

The declaration was ambiguous, balancing the commitment to a Jewish homeland with a promise that "nothing shall be done which may prejudice the civil and religious rights of existing non-Jewish communities in Palestine." This ambiguity, however, sowed the seeds of a protracted conflict. The growing number of Jewish immigrants to Palestine in the subsequent decades, facilitated by British mandate policies, led to mounting tensions and violent clashes between Jewish and Arab communities.

The mandate system in Palestine, Iraq, and Transjordan

The League of Nations mandate system, established after World War I, placed former Ottoman territories under the administration of European powers to prepare them for self-governance. Britain was granted mandates over Palestine, Iraq, and Transjordan, regions of significant strategic and economic interest.

In Palestine, British mandate policies often vacillated between supporting Jewish immigration and attempting to placate Arab opposition. The resulting tensions culminated in widespread violence, such as the Arab Revolt of 1936–1939, and laid the groundwork for the protracted Israeli-Palestinian conflict.

In Iraq, the imposition of a Hashemite monarchy under British auspices created a fragile state structure, plagued by ethnic and sectarian divisions. The legacy of British rule in Iraq includes a history of coups, authoritarian regimes, and ongoing conflicts that have destabilized the region.

Transjordan, later Jordan, emerged as a relatively stable state under the Hashemite monarchy, but the geopolitical ramifications of British policies, particularly regarding the Palestinian issue, continue to influence its politics and security.

Ongoing legacy and regional conflicts

The legacy of the Balfour Declaration and the British mandate system is evident in the persistent conflicts and geopolitical tensions across the Middle East. The creation of the state of Israel in 1948, followed by the Arab Israeli wars, the displacement of Palestinian refugees, and the ongoing struggle for Palestinian statehood, can be traced back to the decisions made during the mandate period.

The arbitrary borders and administrative structures imposed by British rule have left a legacy of fragmented states, each grappling with internal divisions and external pressures. The consequences of these choices serve as evidence of how imperial policies can have far-reaching impacts, highlighting the necessity of comprehending history to confront current challenges.

In conclusion, the Scramble for Africa, the Balfour Declaration, and the British mandate system in the Middle East exemplify the catastrophic decisions made by the British Empire. Driven by a blend of strategic, economic, and ideological motivations, these decisions have left an indelible mark on the political and social landscapes of the affected regions. The more we analyze these and other case studies, the more we will discover the intricate nature and long-lasting consequences of British imperialism.

CHAPTER 5

THE INDIAN SUBCONTINENT

The Kashmir conflict and British policy failures

Stemming from India's 1947 British-orchestrated division, the Kashmir conflict remains one of the most protracted and volatile disputes in the Indian subcontinent. The autonomous region of Jammu and Kashmir, characterized by its Muslim-dominated demographics but led by a Hindu sovereign, evolved into a hotbed of strife between the nascent states of India and Pakistan.

The origins of the Kashmir conflict lie in the hurried and poorly planned British withdrawal from India. While intended to prevent civil war, the decision to split the subcontinent along religious lines triggered one of the most extensive mass migrations in history and widespread communal violence. The Maharaja of Kashmir, Hari Singh, faced immense pressure to choose between joining India or Pakistan. His decision to agree to India, prompted by an invasion of tribal militias from Pakistan, led to the first Indo-Pakistani war.

British policies and their execution during the partition process significantly contributed to the complexity of the Kashmir issue. The arbitrary drawing of borders by Sir Cyril Radcliffe, often without adequate local consultation, resulted in geopolitical fault lines that persist to this day. The British failed to provide a clear and fair process for the integration of princely states, leading to ambiguities and disputes.

Ongoing implications for regional security and Indo-Pakistani relations

The Kashmir conflict has had implications for regional security in South Asia. The unresolved status of Kashmir has led to multiple wars between India and Pakistan, including those in 1947–1948, 1965, and 1999 (the Kargil conflict). Both nations have heavily militarized the region, with frequent skirmishes and ceasefire violations along the Line of Control.

The conflict has also fueled a protracted insurgency within Indian-administered Kashmir, marked by human rights abuses and significant loss of life. The presence of militant groups, some allegedly supported by Pakistan, has further complicated the situation, leading to international concerns about terrorism and nuclear security.

The India-Pakistan struggle over Kashmir has hindered bilateral relations, affecting trade, cultural exchanges, and diplomatic engagement. The conflict has also influenced their respective foreign policies, with both countries seeking strategic alliances and military support from global powers, thus impacting broader regional dynamics.

The Radcliffe Line and its impact on communities

The Radcliffe Line, serving as the demarcation between India and Pakistan, epitomizes the arbitrary and hasty nature of the British partition. Drawn by Cyril Radcliffe, a British lawyer with no prior experience in India, the line cut through villages, farmlands, and communities, creating a legacy of division and displacement.

The immediate impact of the Radcliffe Line was the forced migration of millions of people across the newly drawn borders. Hindus and Sikhs moved from Pakistan to India, while Muslims traveled in the opposite direction. This mass exodus was accompanied by horrific violence, with estimates of up to two million people killed and countless others subjected to atrocities.

The partition not only disrupted lives but also had long-lasting economic and social consequences. Communities that had coexisted for centuries were torn apart, leading to deep-seated mistrust and hatred. The division also disrupted trade routes, economic activities, and familial ties—effects that are still felt today.

The arbitrary nature of the Radcliffe Line is evident in regions such as Punjab and Bengal, where it divides culturally and linguistically homogeneous areas. In Punjab, the division led to significant demographic changes, with the population restructuring along religious lines. In Bengal, the partition created East Pakistan (now Bangladesh) and West Bengal in India, leading to decades of political and economic upheaval.

The Kashmir conflict and the partition of India underscore the catastrophic impact of British policies on the Indian subcontinent. The legacy of these decisions continues to shape regional security, political dynamics, and inter-community relations to this day. As we explore further, we will see how these decisions fit into the broader context of British imperialism and its long-term consequences.

CHAPTER 6

AFRICA

The Mau Mau Uprising and British response

The Mau Mau Uprising (1952–1961) in Kenya was a pivotal event in the history of British colonialism in Africa. It was a rebellion by the Kikuyu people against British colonial rule and the socio-economic injustices it imposed. The uprising highlighted the deep resentment among Kenyans toward land dispossession, forced labor, and the lack of political representation.

The British strategy during the Mau Mau Uprising was characterized by a brutal campaign of suppression. The colonial government declared a state of emergency, detaining tens of thousands of Kikuyu in concentration camps where torture, forced labor, and executions were rampant. The British employed a scorched earth policy, destroying villages and crops to break the will of the insurgents.

The Mau Mau Uprising exposed the moral and political contradictions of British colonial rule. While Britain portrayed itself as a civilized force, its response to the rebellion revealed the extent to which it would go to maintain control and protect settler interests. The human rights abuses committed during the suppression of the uprising have left a lasting scar on Kenyan society.

The Nigerian Civil War and ethnic tensions

The Nigerian Civil War (1967–1971), also known as the Biafran War, was another significant conflict rooted in the legacy of British colonial policies. The arbitrary borders drawn by the British amalgamated diverse ethnic groups—primarily the Hausa-Fulani in the north, the Yoruba in the west, and the Igbo in the east—into a single nation-state. This amalgamation, combined with the British policy of indirect rule, exacerbated ethnic tensions and regional disparities.

The unearthing of oil within the Niger Delta further intensified these tensions, with different regions vying for control of the lucrative resource. The declaration of independence by the southeastern region of Biafra, predominantly Igbo, led to a brutal civil war. The Nigerian government, with British and international support, sought to prevent the secession, leading to widespread devastation and a humanitarian crisis marked by famine and civilian suffering.

The Nigerian Civil War highlighted the deep ethnic divisions and the failure of the post-colonial state to create an inclusive political framework. The legacy of the war continues to affect Nigeria's politics, with periodic outbreaks of violence and persistent demands for greater regional autonomy.

Lasting effects on African nation's development

The long-term effects of British colonialism in Africa are evident in the political, economic, and social challenges faced by many African nations. The imposition of artificial borders, the exploitation of resources, and the establishment of extractive economic systems created a legacy of dependency and underdevelopment.

Post-independence, many African nations struggled to establish stable governance structures. The British model of indirect rule often left behind weak central governments and entrenched local power structures, leading to challenges in nation-building and state consolidation. Corruption, nepotism, and political instability became pervasive issues, hindering economic development and social cohesion.

Economically, the focus on resource extraction during the colonial period left African nations with underdeveloped industries and infrastructure. The continued reliance on exporting raw materials made these economies vulnerable to global market fluctuations, perpetuating cycles of poverty and inequality.

Socially, the legacy of colonial education and cultural policies disrupted Indigenous knowledge systems and societal norms. The introduction of Western education, while creating a new elite, often alienated the majority population and exacerbated social stratification.

The Mau Mau Uprising and the Nigerian Civil War are emblematic of the broader challenges and conflicts engendered by British colonialism in Africa. The legacy of these decisions remains a force in directing the continent's trajectory, calling for a detailed reevaluation of colonial histories and their ongoing repercussions.

Part III
Southeast Asia and the Pacific

CHAPTER 7

BRITISH POLICIES IN SOUTHEAST ASIA

The Malayan Emergency and its impact on society

The Malayan Emergency (1948–1960) was a pivotal conflict in Southeast Asia, illustrating the complexities and consequences of British colonial policies in the region. It began with guerrilla warfare between the Commonwealth armed forces and the Malayan National Liberation Army (MNLA), which served as the armed branch of the Malayan Communist Party (MCP). The conflict was fueled by political, economic, and social grievances among the ethnic Chinese population, who were marginalized under British rule.

The British response to the insurgency was multifaceted, involving military, political, and socioeconomic strategies. The Briggs Plan aimed to isolate insurgents by creating heavily guarded villages and relocating rural Chinese into them. While effective in cutting off support for the guerrillas, this strategy also caused significant displacement and hardship for the local population.

The socioeconomic aspect of British policy focused on winning hearts and minds through development projects and reforms aimed at addressing some of the underlying grievances. The genesis of the Federation of Malaya in 1948 and its subsequent path to independence in 1957 were pivotal steps in this process. These moves aimed to establish a political framework that could accommodate the diverse ethnic groups within Malaya and mitigate communist influence.

The societal consequences of the Malayan Emergency were significant and lasting. While the British suppressed the insurgency and paved the way for Malaya's independence, the legacy of forced relocations and the ethnic divisions they exacerbated continued to influence Malaysian politics. The Emergency also highlighted the limits of military solutions to insurgencies and the importance of addressing socioeconomic inequalities and political grievances.

British rule in Burma and the road to independence

British colonial rule in Burma (now Myanmar) began in the mid-nineteenth century and was marked by a series of wars and subsequent annexations. The imposition of British rule disrupted traditional power structures and introduced new administrative and economic systems that were often exploitative and alienating to the Burmese people.

The road to independence in Burma was turbulent. The rise of nationalist movements in the early twentieth century, led by figures such as Aung San, culminated in the struggle against both British and Japanese occupiers during World War II. The postwar period saw intense negotiations and conflicts as Burma sought to extricate itself from colonial rule.

In 1948, Burma achieved independence, but the legacy of British rule left deep divisions within the country. Ethnic minorities, who had been promised autonomy or independence during the colonial period, found themselves excluded from power in the new state, leading to decades of ethnic insurgencies and conflicts.

The long-term implications of British rule in Burma are evident in the ongoing struggles for political stability, ethnic reconciliation, and economic development. The legacy of colonial administrative practices, which often favored certain ethnic groups over others, continues to influence the country's complex sociopolitical landscape.

The creation of Malaysia and ethnic relations

The formation of Malaysia in 1963 was another significant outcome of British colonial policy in Southeast Asia. This federation united Malaya, Singapore, Sabah, and Sarawak into a single political entity. Geopolitical factors, such as the desire to thwart communist influence and ensure regional political stability, influenced the decision to create Malaysia.

However, the creation of Malaysia also brought about complex ethnic dynamics. The diverse population, comprising Malays, Chinese, Indians, and Indigenous groups, faced challenges creating a cohesive national identity. British colonial policies had entrenched ethnic divisions by implementing a system of ethnic quotas and economic preferences that favored the Malay majority.

The expulsion of Singapore from Malaysia in 1965 highlighted the difficulties in managing these ethnic tensions. Singapore's predominantly Chinese population and its political leadership under Lee Kuan Yew clashed with the Malay-dominated federal government, leading to a peaceful but significant separation.

The continuing challenges related to identity and integration in Malaysia reflect the lasting consequences of British colonial policies. The country has made strides in economic development and social integration, but ethnic relations remain a sensitive and complex issue, influenced by the historical legacies of colonial rule.

CHAPTER 8

HONG KONG AND CHINA

The Opium Wars and acquisition of Hong Kong

The Opium Wars (1839–1842 and 1856–1860) were pivotal events that marked the beginning of a significant British presence in China and the acquisition of Hong Kong. The wars were primarily driven by British desires to balance trade deficits with China by exporting Indian opium, leading to widespread addiction and social disruption in China. When the Qing Dynasty attempted to suppress the opium trade, Britain responded with military force, resulting in decisive victories and the imposition of unequal treaties.

The Treaty of Nanking (1842), which concluded the First Opium War, ceded Hong Kong Island to Britain. Subsequent treaties expanded British control over the Kowloon Peninsula and the New Territories, establishing Hong Kong as a key strategic and commercial outpost in Asia. The acquisition of Hong Kong allowed Britain access to the lucrative Chinese market and facilitated the projection of its influence in the region.

Impact on Hong Kong's development and the handover to China

Under British rule, Hong Kong became an important international trade hub and financial center. The colonial administration established robust legal and financial systems, infrastructure, and public services that facilitated rapid economic growth. Hong Kong's free-market policies and strategic location attracted businesses and immigrants, transforming it into a vibrant, cosmopolitan city.

However, British colonial rule also had its limitations. Political participation for the local population was limited, and significant social and economic inequalities persisted. Despite these challenges, the people of Hong Kong developed a unique identity, blending Chinese traditions with British legal and administrative frameworks.

Hong Kong's 1997 reintegration into China, under the framework of "one country, two systems," marked a significant transition. This arrangement was designed to preserve Hong Kong's capitalist system and way of life for fifty years after the handover. The long-term effects of this arrangement are still unfolding, with ongoing tensions between the desire for democratic governance and Beijing's increasing influence.

The legacy of British rule in Hong Kong is multifaceted, characterized by economic success and political complexity. The city's rise as a global financial hub demonstrates its distinctive history, while the current political obstacles underscore the lasting influence of its colonial era.

CHAPTER 9

OCEANIA

Colonization of Australia and New Zealand

The colonization of Australia and New Zealand by the British Empire began in the late eighteenth century, fundamentally transforming the Indigenous societies and landscapes of these regions. The arrival of the First Fleet in 1788 signaled the beginning of British settlement in Australia, initially establishing a penal settlement. Over the subsequent decades, British settlers expanded across the continent, often at the expense of the Aboriginal populations.

The impact on the native populations was devastating. British policies of displacement, assimilation, and land appropriation led to significant loss of life, culture, and autonomy for Aboriginal Australians. The emergence of novel diseases to which Indigenous peoples had no immunity decimated communities. The practice of removing Aboriginal children, known as the Stolen Generations, sought to assimilate them into white society, causing deep social and psychological trauma and social scars that persist today.

The Treaty of Waitangi, signed in 1840, signaled the start of serious British colonization efforts in New Zealand. This treaty, which was meant to establish a framework for British settlement and Māori rights, was interpreted differently by the British and Māori. The subsequent land conflicts, known as the New Zealand Wars, highlighted the tensions between Māori land rights and British colonial expansion.

The impacts of British colonization on Australia's and New Zealand's social and cultural aspects are significant and lasting. Indigenous movements in both countries continue to seek recognition of rights, land restitution, and cultural revival, challenging the legacies of colonial rule.

The Pacific Islands

British influence in the Pacific Islands varied, encompassing both direct colonial rule and informal control. Territories such as Fiji, the Solomon Islands, and the Gilbert and Ellice Islands (now Kiribati and Tuvalu) came under British administration during the late nineteenth and early twentieth centuries.

The impact of colonization on the Pacific Islands included significant social and economic changes. The introduction of cash economies, Christianity, and Western educational systems disrupted traditional societies. The economic impact of exploiting resources and labor, especially in plantation economies, had lasting consequences.

The aftermath of British colonial governance in the Pacific Islands is mixed. While colonial infrastructure and education systems facilitated some development, they also created dependency and disrupted local governance structures. The postcolonial period has seen efforts to revive traditional practices and assert political autonomy, but challenges remain in addressing the inequalities and dependencies established during the colonial era.

To sum up, colonial rule in Southeast Asia and the Pacific evidenced the extensive and frequently destructive effects of British policies. From the forced relocations of the Malayan Emergency to the ongoing struggles for Indigenous rights in Australia and New Zealand, the legacies of British imperialism continue to shape the region. Through further exploration of these themes, we will enhance our understanding of the intricate and long-lasting effects caused by the global expansion of the British Empire.

Part IV

The Caribbean and Ireland

CHAPTER 10

THE CARIBBEAN

The legacy of slavery and socioeconomic impacts

The British Empire's involvement in the Caribbean is deeply entwined with the transatlantic slave trade and the plantation economy. From the seventeenth century onward, British colonies in the Caribbean, such as Jamaica, Barbados, and Trinidad, became hubs for the production of sugar, tobacco, and other cash crops. These plantations were operated through the brutal exploitation of enslaved Africans, who were forcibly transported across the Atlantic in appalling conditions.

The Caribbean continues to bear the weight of slavery's profound legacy. The economic foundations of many Caribbean nations were built on the labor of enslaved people, creating vast wealth for British merchants and plantation owners while subjecting generations of Africans to unimaginable suffering. The abolition of slavery in 1834 did little to alleviate the socioeconomic disparities that had been entrenched by centuries of exploitation.

The socioeconomic impacts of slavery are evident in the persistent inequalities and underdevelopment in many Caribbean societies. The post-emancipation period saw the emergence of a system of indentured labor, primarily drawing workers from India, further complicating the social and ethnic landscape of the Caribbean. The descendants of enslaved Africans and indentured laborers are still dealing with the backlash of colonialism, including land ownership issues, economic disparities, and social stratification.

Efforts at reparations and reconciliation have gained momentum in recent years, with Caribbean nations seeking acknowledgment and redress for the historical injustices of slavery. The Caribbean Community (CARICOM) has been at the forefront of efforts advocating for reparatory justice from former colonial powers.

Colonial governance and independence movements

British colonial governance in the Caribbean was characterized by a rigid hierarchical structure that privileged the interests of the colonial administration and the planter elite over those of the local population. Colonial policies were primarily geared toward maintaining control and maximizing economic output, often at the expense of social and political development.

The struggle for independence in the Caribbean was marked by both peaceful negotiations and violent uprisings. Figures such as Marcus Garvey and later political leaders like Sir Alexander Bustamante in Jamaica and Eric Williams in Trinidad and Tobago played crucial roles in mobilizing anti-colonial sentiments and advocating for self-governance.

The postcolonial challenges faced by Caribbean nations were complex. Newly independent states had to navigate the complexities of building national identities in ethnically diverse societies, addressing economic dependencies on former colonial powers, and establishing stable political institutions. The vestiges of colonial dominance, including constrained economic diversity and ingrained social hierarchies, continue to direct the developmental trajectories of Caribbean states.

In summary, the British Empire's legacy in the Caribbean is one of deep-seated socioeconomic inequality and a prolonged struggle for political and economic autonomy. The region's narrative of slavery, colonial exploitation, and the subsequent fight for independence underscores the lingering aftermath of British imperial policies.

CHAPTER 11

IRELAND

The partition of Ireland and its impact

The fragmentation of Ireland in 1921, giving rise to Northern Ireland and the Irish Free State (later the Republic of Ireland), stands as another momentous and controversial action taken by the British Empire. The roots of partition lie in the complex interplay of political, religious, and nationalistic forces that have shaped Irish history for centuries.

The Government of Ireland Act 1920, enacted by the British Parliament, effectively divided the island into two separate entities. Northern Ireland, with its Protestant majority, remained part of the United Kingdom, while the Catholic south became a separate entity, eventually gaining complete independence as the Republic of Ireland.

The partition of Ireland had immediate and long-term impacts on the island's political and social landscape. In Northern Ireland, the division entrenched sectarian divisions and laid the groundwork for decades of conflict, known as "The Troubles," which erupted in the late 1960s. This period of intense sectarian violence between Protestant unionists, who wanted to remain part of the UK, and Catholic nationalists, who sought reunification with the Republic of Ireland, resulted in significant loss of life and deep social scars.

The consequences on Northern Ireland and the Republic of Ireland have been substantial. In Northern Ireland, the conflict has shaped its political, social, and economic development, while the Republic of Ireland has had to navigate its relationship with its northern neighbor and the broader implications for Irish nationalism and identity.

The Troubles and their long-term legacy

The Troubles, extending from the late 1960s until the Good Friday Agreement in 1998, were noted for their violent conflicts, bomb explosions, and a wave of assassinations. The British military presence in Northern Ireland, intended to restore order, often exacerbated tensions and led to accusations of human rights abuses.

The Good Friday Agreement, a landmark peace deal, brought an end to the most intense period of violence and established a framework for power-sharing and political cooperation in Northern Ireland. However, the long-term legacy of the Troubles continues to influence Northern Ireland's politics and society. Sectarian divisions remain, and occasional outbreaks of violence remind us of the fragility of the peace process.

The British policies that led to the partition of Ireland and the subsequent handling of the Troubles highlight the complexities and challenges of colonial governance. The ramifications of these policies continues to affect Anglo-Irish relations and the pursuit of lasting peace and reconciliation in Northern Ireland.

In conclusion, the British Empire's influence in the Caribbean and Ireland showcases the extensive and often detrimental impacts of colonial policies. From the economic exploitation and social upheaval in the Caribbean to the sectarian violence and political divisions in Ireland, the legacies of British rule continue to shape these regions' contemporary realities.

Part V

Thematic Analyses

CHAPTER 12

ECONOMIC EXPLOITATION AND GLOBAL TRADE NETWORKS

Exploitation of resources and economic policies

The economic policies of the British Empire were designed fundamentally to extract maximum wealth from its colonies and integrate them into a global trade network that prioritized British monetary interests. This exploitation of resources, whether through agriculture, mining, or other industries, had lasting impacts on the colonies' economies and environments.

In India, the British implemented policies that transformed the agrarian economy to serve British industrial needs. The proliferation of market-oriented crops like cotton and indigo eclipsed the production of traditional food-yielding vegetation, instigating sporadic hunger crises when harvests underperformed. The exploitation of India's textile industry, once a global leader, left the country's weavers impoverished as British manufactured goods flooded the market, undermining local industries.

In Africa, the extraction of minerals, rubber, and other resources underpinned the colonial economy. The imposition of cash crops and forced labor systems disrupted traditional economies and societies. The economic policies in colonies like Nigeria, Ghana, and South Africa were geared toward benefiting the colonial powers, leaving a legacy of financial dependency and underdevelopment.

The Caribbean exemplified the extraction of wealth through the exploitation of enslaved and indentured labor. The sugar and tobacco industries generated immense profits for British merchants and planters, while the local populations endured harsh working conditions and systemic inequalities.

Long-term economic challenges in former colonies

The long-term economic challenges faced by former colonies are deeply rooted in the legacy of British exploitation. Many former colonies have struggled to diversify their economies, which were heavily reliant on the extraction and export of raw materials. This dependency on global commodity markets has made these economies vulnerable to price fluctuations and economic instability.

Post-independence, many former colonies inherited economic structures that favored the elite and foreign interests, perpetuating inequalities. The lack of investment in local industries and infrastructure left these nations with significant developmental challenges. Efforts to industrialize and develop have often been hampered by the need to service debts incurred during and after colonial rule.

In addition to economic challenges, the environmental degradation caused by colonial exploitation continues to impact former colonies. The deforestation, soil depletion, and pollution resulting from resource extraction have had long-term consequences for agriculture and livelihoods.

Comparative insights from other empires

The economic exploitation by the British Empire can be compared to similar practices by other colonial powers. The French, Dutch, and Spanish empires also implemented policies prioritizing wealth extraction from their colonies, often leading to similar long-term economic challenges.

However, the British Empire's scale and reach, coupled with its particular strategies of indirect rule and economic integration, created unique impacts. The British had a unique approach to creating global trade networks and integrating colonies into the world economy, significantly influencing the economic development of their former territories.

The economic exploitation by the British Empire created enduring challenges for its former colonies. The extraction of resources and the imposition of economic policies that prioritized British interests left a legacy of dependency, underdevelopment, and environmental degradation.

CHAPTER 13

EDUCATION AND CULTURAL POLICIES

British educational systems and their impact on local cultures

The introduction of British educational systems in the colonies was a central aspect of the imperial project, reflecting the belief in the civilizing mission of the Empire. British education aimed to instill Western values, knowledge, and languages, ostensibly to prepare colonial subjects for administrative roles and to promote modernity. However, this imposition had profound and often detrimental impacts on local cultures and societies.

In India, the implementation of English education began in earnest with Lord Macaulay's Minute on Indian Education in 1835, which advocated for the promotion of English as the medium of instruction. This policy aimed to create a class of "brown Englishmen" educated in British values and capable of serving the colonial administration. While English education provided opportunities for social mobility and produced a Westernized elite, it also displaced traditional forms of knowledge and education, leading to a cultural disconnection for many Indians.

In Africa, missionary schools played a significant role in spreading Western education. These institutions frequently prioritized religious instruction alongside basic literacy and numeracy, with the dual aim of converting local populations to Christianity and promoting Western cultural norms. The emphasis on European history, literature, and science often came at the expense of the knowledge and languages of original inhabitants, contributing to the erosion of local cultural identities.

The British educational policies in the Caribbean, Australia, and New Zealand similarly aimed to inculcate Western values and knowledge. In the Caribbean, education systems reinforced colonial hierarchies and often excluded Afro-Caribbean cultural heritage from the curriculum. In Australia and New Zealand, the education of Indigenous peoples was geared toward assimilation, with curricula designed to undermine traditional cultures and languages.

Policies aimed at cultural assimilation and suppression

The British Empire's cultural policies were typically aimed at assimilation and suppression of local traditions and identities. These policies sought to replace the cultural practices of native peoples with British norms and values, reinforcing the notion of Western superiority.

In India, cultural assimilation was pursued through various means, including the promotion of English education and the suppression of traditional practices deemed "barbaric" or "backward" by the British. The banning of practices such as sati (widow burning) and the reform of Hindu and Muslim personal laws were part of broader efforts to reshape Indian society along Western lines. While some reforms were motivated by genuine humanitarian concerns, they were also used to justify colonial rule and assert British moral authority.

In Africa, the suppression of cultural practices was closely tied to missionary activities and colonial governance. Traditional religious practices, rituals, and social structures were often dismissed as primitive and targeted for eradication. The introduction of Western dress, customs, and Christian names further aimed to assimilate African populations into a colonial mold.

In Australia and New Zealand, policies of cultural suppression were harsh toward Indigenous populations. The Stolen Generations in Australia, where Aboriginal children were forcibly taken from their families and placed in institutions or foster homes to assimilate them into white society, exemplify these policies. The Tohunga Suppression Act of 1907 in New Zealand aimed to eradicate Māori traditional healing practices, reflecting broader efforts to diminish Māori cultural autonomy.

Ongoing struggles for cultural revival and recognition

The legacy of British educational and cultural policies has had lasting impacts on former colonies, leading to ongoing struggles for cultural revival and recognition. In many postcolonial societies, there has been a concerted effort to reclaim and revitalize the cultures and traditions of oppressed groups that were suppressed or silenced during the colonial period.

In India, there has been a resurgence of interest in traditional knowledge systems, languages, and cultural practices. Initiatives to incorporate Indigenous knowledge into the formal education system and to promote regional languages reflect a broader movement toward cultural decolonization. Cultural festivals, literature, and media increasingly celebrate India's diverse heritage, challenging the hegemony of colonial-era narratives.

In Africa, the postcolonial period has seen efforts to revive traditional practices and knowledge systems. Educational reforms have aimed to incorporate Indigenous languages and histories into curricula, while cultural revival movements seek to restore and celebrate African heritage. These efforts are part of broader struggles for cultural and political autonomy, challenging the legacies of colonial rule.

In the Caribbean, the recognition and celebration of Afro-Caribbean culture have been central to national identity and postcolonial development. Cultural forms such as reggae music, calypso, and carnival have become symbols of resistance and resilience, reflecting the region's complex history and diverse heritage. Educational initiatives increasingly emphasize the importance of local history and cultural heritage, seeking to redress the colonial emphasis on European traditions.

Indigenous cultural revival has been a pivotal element in the struggle for recognition and rights in Australia and New Zealand. In Australia, movements to acknowledge and rectify the injustices of the Stolen Generations, along with efforts to revive Aboriginal languages and cultural practices, are central to the broader reconciliation process. In New Zealand, the revival of Te Reo Māori, the Māori language, and the recognition of Māori cultural practices within national institutions reflect significant strides toward cultural reclamation and empowerment.

The impact of British educational and cultural policies on former colonies has resulted in a complex legacy. While these policies brought Western knowledge and values, they also actively suppressed and undermined the cultural practices of native populations. The ongoing efforts to revive and recognize local traditions and knowledge systems highlight the far-reaching effects of colonial rule and the resilience of colonized peoples to reclaim their cultural identities.

CHAPTER 14

HEALTH AND DEMOGRAPHIC CHANGES

The advent of British colonial rule across diverse regions of the world brought profound changes, particularly in the realm of health and demographics. One of the most significant impacts was the introduction of new diseases to Indigenous populations who had no prior exposure to or immunity to them. This phenomenon led to devastating epidemics and long-term health crises in many colonies.

In the Americas, introducing diseases such as smallpox, measles, and influenza by European settlers decimated Indigenous populations. These diseases spread rapidly, killing millions, and contributing to the collapse of established societies and cultures. In other global regions, like Australia and the Pacific Islands, analogous patterns emerged, where the introduction of diseases led to catastrophic declines in in the populations of original inhabitants.

The British responses to these health crises varied. In some instances, efforts were made to control and mitigate the spread of diseases through vaccination campaigns and public health measures.

Smallpox vaccination, for example, was promoted in several colonies. However, these efforts were often inconsistent and inadequate, particularly in the face of widespread epidemics and limited medical infrastructure.

The British colonial administration regularly prioritized the health of European settlers and military personnel over that of the local population. Medical services were regularly concentrated in urban centers and areas of strategic importance, leaving rural and remote communities with little access to healthcare. This disparity exacerbated the impact of diseases and contributed to long-term health inequalities.

Population displacement and migration patterns

The British Empire's expansion and the economic policies it implemented led to significant population displacement and migration, reshaping the demographic landscape of many regions. The social and economic impacts of the forced movement of people were substantial, whether it was through the transatlantic slave trade, indentured labor systems, or internal displacements.

The transatlantic slave trade, which mercilessly uprooted millions of Africans to the Americas, was one of the most brutal forms of population displacement. Enslaved Africans were subjected to inhumane conditions and harsh labor, fundamentally altering the demographic and cultural composition of the Caribbean, North America, and parts of South America. The prolonged shadow of the slave trade continues to impact these regions, contributing to racial and social inequalities.

In the Indian subcontinent, British economic strategies and infrastructure undertakings, including the construction of railways and the establishment of plantations, caused considerable internal displacement. Additionally, the British colonial administration facilitated the migration of Indian laborers to other parts of the Empire, including the Caribbean, Southeast Asia, and Africa, under the indentured labor system. These laborers, often facing harsh conditions and exploitation, established diasporic communities that continue to influence the cultural and demographic makeup of their respective regions.

In 1947, the partition of India resulted in one of the largest mass migrations in history. The hastily drawn Radcliffe Line led to the displacement of approximately fourteen million people along religious lines, causing widespread communal violence, loss of life, and long-term demographic shifts. The partition not only reshaped the population distribution in South Asia but also left deep scars and ongoing conflicts, particularly over the disputed region of Kashmir.

Long-term health and demographic impacts

The long-term health and demographic impacts of British colonial policies are multifaceted and continue to influence former colonies today. The introduction of new diseases and inadequate healthcare responses led to lasting health disparities and vulnerabilities. The displacement and migration patterns orchestrated by the British created complex demographic mosaics that continue to shape social, economic, and political dynamics.

In many former colonies, the legacy of colonial healthcare systems persists in the form of unequal access to medical services and health infrastructure. Historical neglect and the prioritization of colonial urban centers are evident in the limited healthcare access for rural and marginalized communities. Efforts to address these disparities are ongoing, but the structural challenges rooted in colonial history remain significant obstacles.

The demographic changes induced by forced migrations and displacements have also had enduring effects. The diasporic communities established during the colonial period have contributed to the cultural diversity of many regions, but they also face challenges related to integration, identity, and socioeconomic inequalities. The historical injustices and traumas associated with these movements continue to influence contemporary debates on migration, citizenship, and human rights.

The British Empire profoundly and often devastatingly impacted health and demographics in its colonies through practices such as the spread of new diseases, forced relocations, and manipulated migration. These colonial actions have left indelible marks on the health and demographic landscapes of former colonies.

Part VI

Legal and Administrative Legacies

CHAPTER 15

LEGAL SYSTEMS AND ADMINISTRATIVE POLICIES

Introduction of British legal systems and their conflicts with local laws

The imposition of British legal systems across the Empire was a fundamental aspect of colonial administration, often clashing with existing legal traditions and practices. The introduction of English common law and statutory codes aimed to create a uniform legal framework but frequently displaced existing legal practices.

The Indian Penal Code and the Criminal Procedure Code are two examples of how British legal reforms in India established a centralized judicial system. These laws aimed to standardize legal practices and introduce principles of fairness and justice. However, they frequently disregarded local customs and traditional dispute-resolution mechanisms. The codification of legal statutes led to the erosion of customary laws and created a disconnect between the legal system and the societal norms of many communities.

In Africa, the British implemented a dual legal system, combining colonial and customary laws. This approach, particularly prevalent in Nigeria and Kenya, sought to accommodate local customs while asserting colonial authority. However, the integration was often uneven, with British laws taking precedence, leading to tensions and conflicts between the two systems. The result was a fragmented legal landscape that continues to affect governance and justice in many African countries.

In the Caribbean, the transplantation of British legal principles established a framework that emphasized property rights and commercial law, reflecting the economic priorities of the colonial administration. Social justice and equity faced long-term challenges due to the legal systems in these colonies, which typically upheld social hierarchies and economic inequalities.

Examination of administrative structures and governance

The British administrative structures were designed to efficiently maintain control over vast and diverse territories. This often involved a combination of direct and indirect rules tailored to each colony's specific context.

In India, the British established a centralized bureaucracy through the Indian Civil Service (ICS), which was the backbone of colonial administration. British officers occupied key positions, ensuring tight control over the administration. This centralized system left little room for Indian participation, fostering resentment, and fueling nationalist movements.

In contrast, the British employed indirect rule in many African colonies, governing through local leaders and traditional authorities. This system, articulated by Lord Lugard, aimed to minimize administrative costs, and maintain order by co-opting existing power structures. While it allowed for a semblance of local autonomy, it also entrenched traditional hierarchies and often led to manipulation and corruption. The legacy of indirect rule has had lasting effects on governance, contributing to issues of political fragmentation and weak state institutions.

In colonized territories like Australia, Canada, and New Zealand, British administrative policies focused on establishing local self-governance structures that eventually evolved into independent nation-states. However, these policies also resulted in the marginalization and displacement of native populations, creating long-term social and economic disparities.

Lasting influence on contemporary legal and administrative systems

The legal and administrative legacies of the British Empire continue to shape governance in former colonies. Many countries retain legal systems and institutions rooted in their colonial past. The common law system, with its principles of judicial precedent and procedural fairness, remains central to legal practice in countries such as India, Pakistan, Nigeria, and Kenya.

However, the transplantation of British legal systems has also created challenges. The disconnect between formal legal institutions and customary practices often leads to conflicts and inefficiencies. In many former colonies, legal systems are perceived as alien and inaccessible, resulting in a lack of trust and engagement with formal judicial processes.

The administrative legacies of the British Empire are equally significant. Centralized control, bureaucratic governance, and the legacy of indirect rule have influenced the development of governance structures. Issues such as centralized power, a lack of local autonomy, and bureaucratic inefficiencies can frequently be traced back to colonial administrative practices.

The British Empire's imposition of legal systems and administrative structures has had a long-lasting and intricate impact. While British legal principles and administrative models continue to shape contemporary governance, they also pose significant challenges, reflecting colonial rule's deep-seated and often contentious impacts. As we move forward, we will explore the broader social, cultural, and political implications of these legacies, examining how they intersect with the economic and geopolitical dimensions of British imperialism.

CHAPTER 16

SOCIAL AND HUMAN RIGHTS ISSUES

British policies that entrenched social hierarchies and class divisions

The British Empire's administrative and social policies were designed to entrench and perpetuate social hierarchies and class divisions within their colonies. These policies were rooted in the belief in the inherent superiority of British culture and institutions, which justified the domination and exploitation of colonized peoples.

In India, the British reinforced existing social hierarchies, particularly the caste system, to maintain control. The policy of divide and rule aimed to fragment Indian society by fostering divisions among various religious, ethnic, and social groups. The British codification of caste in the census and their preferential treatment of certain castes over others entrenched these divisions and exacerbated social stratification. This policy had long-lasting effects, as caste-based discrimination continued to affect social dynamics and economic opportunities even after independence.

In Africa, British policies often reinforced tribal divisions and ethnic hierarchies. The practice of indirect rule, which was governed by traditional leaders, entrenched the power of certain ethnic groups while marginalizing others. This approach not only maintained colonial control but also sowed the seeds of ethnic conflicts and political instability that have persisted in many African nations.

In the Caribbean, the plantation economy established by the British created a rigid class system based on race and ethnicity. Enslaved Africans and their descendants were at the bottom of the social hierarchy, while white planters and colonial administrators occupied the top tiers. After the abolition of slavery, the introduction of indentured labor from India and China created additional layers of social stratification. These hierarchies were reinforced through legal and social structures, leading to deep-rooted racial and economic inequalities that persist today.

Examination of human rights abuses under British rule

The British Empire's history is replete with instances of human rights abuses, often carried out in the name of maintaining order and expanding control. These abuses took various forms, including violence, forced labor, land dispossession, and the suppression of dissent.

In Kenya, the suppression of the Mau Mau Uprising involved widespread human rights abuses. The British colonial government established detention camps where suspected Mau Mau supporters were subjected to torture, forced labor, and extrajudicial killings. The systematic brutality used to suppress the uprising left a lasting legacy of trauma and injustice among the Kikuyu people.

In India, the Amritsar Massacre of 1919 stands out as a stark example of British brutality. British troops, led by General Reginald Dyer, opened fire upon a peaceful assembly in Jallianwala Bagh, killing hundreds of unarmed civilians. This atrocity galvanized the Indian independence movement and highlighted the repressive nature of British rule.

The transatlantic slave trade, heavily driven by the British, was one of the most egregious human rights abuses in history. Countless Africans were violently uprooted and shipped to the Americas in appalling circumstances, subjected to savage mistreatment and stripped of their fundamental human dignities. The legacy of slavery continues to impact descendants of enslaved peoples through systemic racism and socioeconomic disadvantages.

The displacement and marginalization of Indigenous populations in Australia and New Zealand also involved significant human rights abuses. Policies of land dispossession, cultural assimilation, and forced removal of children from their families (such as the Stolen Generations in Australia) inflicted severe social and psychological harm. These policies sought to eradicate Indigenous cultures and identities, resulting in a legacy of intergenerational trauma and persistent struggles for justice and recognition.

Long-term impact on justice and reconciliation processes

The human rights abuses committed under British rule have had long-term impacts on justice and reconciliation processes in former colonies. Addressing these historical injustices remains a complex and ongoing challenge.

In Kenya, the survivors of the Mau Mau Uprising have sought justice through legal avenues. In 2013, the British government issued an official apology and agreed to compensate thousands of Kenyans who experienced torture and abuse during the uprising. This acknowledgment was a significant step toward reconciliation, but many victims and their descendants continue to seek full justice and recognition of their suffering.

In India, the legacy of British rule, including events like the Amritsar Massacre, continues to shape national memory and identity. The demand for an official apology from the British government for colonial-era atrocities remains a point of contention in Indo-British relations. Efforts to document and memorialize these events are part of broader attempts to reckon with the colonial past and its lasting impacts.

The historical legacy of racial discrimination and slavery in the Caribbean has spurred movements for reparations and social justice. The Caribbean Community has been actively pursuing reparations from European nations for the damage caused by slavery and colonial exploitation. These efforts aim to address historical injustices and promote economic and social development in the region.

Reconciliation efforts with Indigenous populations have been ongoing in Australia and New Zealand. Significant steps in Australia include National Sorry Day and the establishment of the National Apology in 2008, which aimed to acknowledge the injustices faced by Aboriginal and Torres Strait Islander peoples. Meanwhile, in New Zealand, the Treaty of Waitangi settlements process seeks to address historical grievances and restore Māori rights and resources.

To sum up, the British Empire's policies entrenched social hierarchies perpetrated human rights abuses and left a legacy of injustice and inequality. The far-reaching effects of these policies continue to shape contemporary struggles for justice and reconciliation in former colonies. Understanding and addressing these historical legacies is crucial for fostering healing and building more equitable societies.

Part VII

Resistance, Rebellion, and Postcolonial Challenges

CHAPTER 17

ANTI-COLONIAL MOVEMENTS AND REBELLIONS

The history of the British Empire is rich with resistance and rebellion, as colonized peoples sought to overthrow imperial dominance and reclaim their autonomy. These movements were driven by economic exploitation, cultural suppression, and a desire for self-determination.

One of the most notable resistance movements was the Indian independence movement, spearheaded by influential figures like Subhas Chandra Bose, Mahatma Gandhi, and Jawaharlal Nehru. Gandhi's philosophy of nonviolent resistance, or Satyagraha, mobilized millions against British rule. Key events such as the Non-Cooperation Movement (1920–1922), the Salt March (1930), and the Quit India Movement (1942) were instrumental in weakening British control and galvanizing Indian nationalism. The eventual withdrawal of the British in 1947 and the subsequent partition into India and Pakistan were outcomes of this sustained struggle.

In Africa, anti-colonial resistance varied from peaceful protests to armed insurrections. The Mau Mau Uprising was a major armed rebellion against colonial rule, fueled by grievances over land dispossession and social inequality. Despite the brutal suppression by the British, which included mass detentions and human rights abuses, the uprising intensified international and domestic pressure for decolonization, leading to Kenya's independence in 1963.

In Ghana, Kwame Nkrumah led a successful nonviolent campaign for independence, founding the Convention People's Party (CPP) and advocating for Pan-African unity. Ghana's independence in 1957 was a landmark event that inspired other African nations to pursue their liberation.

In the Caribbean, resistance manifested through both revolts and intellectual movements. Although the Haitian Revolution (1791–1804) was not directly under British control, it had a profound impact on antislavery and anti-colonial sentiments in the region. The labor riots of the 1930s in Jamaica, Trinidad, and other islands catalyzed political reforms and the rise of nationalist leaders, who eventually led their countries to independence in the mid-twentieth century.

Long-term impacts on national identities and postcolonial state formation

The anti-colonial movements significantly shaped national identities and the process of state formation in former colonies. These movements fostered a sense of unity and collective identity that was crucial for nation-building in the postcolonial period.

In India, the independence movement's emphasis on pluralism and secularism influenced framing of the Indian Constitution and the establishment of democratic institutions. However, the traumatic partition and subsequent conflicts over Kashmir highlighted the religious and ethnic divides exacerbated by colonial rule, posing ongoing challenges to national unity.

In Africa, the legacy of resistance movements was mixed. While they played a critical role in achieving independence, the newly formed states often inherited colonial boundaries and administrative structures that did not align with pre-colonial ethnic and cultural realities. This misalignment has led to persistent ethnic tensions, political instability, and struggles with governance.

In the Caribbean, the legacy of slavery and colonial exploitation shaped national identities and sociopolitical structures. The struggle for emancipation and equality became central themes in the post-colonial narrative, influencing cultural expressions and political agendas. Leaders like Marcus Garvey and later political figures in independent Caribbean nations emphasized the importance of Afro-Caribbean identity and cultural pride.

Case studies: Indian Independence Movement, Mau Mau Uprising, Haitian Revolution

The Indian independence movement exemplifies the power of nonviolent resistance and the mobilization of mass support. Gandhi's campaigns against British policies, such as the boycott of British goods and the Salt March, effectively highlighted the injustices of colonial rule and garnered international sympathy. The movement's success in achieving independence set a precedent for other colonies and underscored the importance of political unity and strategic nonviolence.

The Mau Mau Uprising in Kenya illustrated the complexities of armed resistance. While it exposed the brutality of colonial repression and galvanized international support for decolonization, it also led to significant human suffering and divisions within Kenyan society. The uprising's legacy is a reminder of the high costs of violent resistance and the long-term challenges of reconciliation and nation-building.

The Haitian Revolution was a pioneering anti-colonial and anti-slavery struggle that left a lasting mark on global history. The successful overthrow of French colonial rule by enslaved Africans in Haiti established the first Black republic and sent shockwaves through the colonial world. Despite the severe economic and political isolation that the colonial powers imposed on Haiti, it demonstrated the possibility for enslaved peoples to achieve liberation and motivated subsequent resistance movements.

CHAPTER 18

POSTCOLONIAL TRANSITIONS AND ECONOMIC DEPENDENCY

Challenges faced by former colonies in transitioning to independence

The shift from colonial dominance to independence was fraught with numerous challenges for former British colonies. These challenges were multifaceted, encompassing political, economic, and social dimensions that required newly independent states to navigate complex and often hostile environments.

One of the primary challenges was establishing stable governance structures. Many colonies inherited administrative frameworks designed to serve colonial interests rather than local needs. The lack of experience in self-governance, coupled with artificial borders that often ignored ethnic and cultural realities, led to political instability and conflict. In Africa, for example, the arbitrary boundaries drawn by colonial powers contributed to ethnic tensions and civil wars in countries like Nigeria, Sudan, and Rwanda.

The political vacuum left by the departing British typically resulted in power struggles and coups as different factions vied for control. The Cold War context further complicated these transitions, with the United States and the Soviet Union competing for influence in newly independent states. This geopolitical rivalry frequently exacerbated internal conflicts and hindered efforts to establish stable and inclusive governments.

Economically, the transition to independence was equally challenging. Colonial economies were typically geared toward extracting and exporting raw materials to the metropole, resulting in a lack of industrial infrastructure and economic diversification. The departure of colonial administrators and European settlers often led to a sudden loss of technical expertise and capital, further straining the nascent economies of newly independent states.

Socially, colonial rule's legacy left deep divisions within societies. The entrenchment of social hierarchies and class divisions, regularly along racial or ethnic lines, continued to influence post-colonial societies. These entrenched divisions hampered efforts to forge national identities and foster social cohesion, resulting in ongoing struggles for harmony and justice.

Examination of economic policies that created dependency on Britain

The economic policies implemented during British colonial rule were designed to integrate colonies into the global economy in ways that benefited the British metropole. These policies often created economic dependencies that persisted long after independence.

In many colonies, the emphasis was on extracting and exporting a few primary commodities, including minerals, cash crops, and other raw materials. This focus on monoculture economies made colonies highly prone to fluctuations in world market prices and left them with limited economic diversification. For example, the reliance on cotton in India, rubber in Malaya, and cocoa in Ghana created economies that depended heavily on the export of these commodities.

The British also established trade patterns that favored the metropole. Colonies were encouraged, or in some cases, compelled, to import manufactured goods from Britain, leading to a trade imbalance that favored the British economy. This trade pattern inhibited the development of local industries and created a dependency on British goods and capital.

Financial policies during colonial rule further entrenched economic dependency. Colonial administrations frequently depended on British investment for infrastructure projects, which created debt dependencies. The financial systems established in the colonies were designed to ensure profits were repatriated to Britain rather than reinvested in local economies. This wealth extraction hindered economic development and left newly independent states with significant financial challenges.

In addition, the education systems established by the British often emphasized administrative and clerical skills needed for colonial administration rather than technical and industrial skills necessary for economic development. This focus limited the capacity of newly independent states to develop the human capital required for diversified economic growth.

Long-term economic challenges in former colonies

The economic legacy of British colonial rule has created long-term challenges for former colonies, many of which still grapple with underdevelopment, poverty, and inequality.

One of the most significant long-term challenges has been the lack of economic diversification. Many former colonies remain dependent on the export of a limited range of primary commodities, making them vulnerable to global market volatility. This lack of diversification hampers economic resilience and growth, contributing to persistent poverty and inequality.

The infrastructure in many former colonies was developed to serve colonial interests, typically focusing on resource extraction and export rather than comprehensive national development. As a result, many countries are left with inadequate transportation, energy, and communication infrastructure, which hinders economic development and their integration into the global economy.

Debt dependency is another critical issue. Many former colonies emerged from the colonial period with significant debt burdens, often incurred to finance infrastructure projects that primarily benefited the colonial powers. These debt burdens have restricted economic growth and curtailed the ability of governments to invest in social and economic development.

The legacy of trade imbalances also continues to affect former colonies. The established patterns of trade, favoring exporting raw materials and importing manufactured goods, have been challenging to break. Attempts to develop local industries and achieve greater economic self-sufficiency have frequently been impeded by entrenched trade relationships.

Furthermore, the social legacies of colonial rule, including entrenched social hierarchies and class divisions, continue to influence economic opportunities and outcomes. Inequalities in land ownership, access to education, and economic opportunities remain significant barriers to inclusive development.

In summary, the transition to independence for former British colonies was characterized by significant challenges, especially in establishing stable governance structures and achieving economic self-sufficiency. The economic policies implemented during colonial rule created dependencies that have persisted, posing long-term obstacles to development. Mitigating these historical challenges requires concerted action on economic diversity, infrastructure development, and social equity, mindful of British colonialism's lasting imprint.

Part VIII

Interdisciplinary and Comparative Perspectives

CHAPTER 19

HISTORICAL, SOCIOLOGICAL, AND ECONOMIC ANALYSES

Historians have provided invaluable insights into the long-term impacts of British imperial policies on former colonies. These analyses highlight the complexity and breadth of the empire's legacy, encompassing political, social, economic, and cultural dimensions.

Historians such as Niall Ferguson have asserted that the British Empire was instrumental in promoting global trade, establishing legal systems, and building infrastructure, which, they contend, laid the groundwork for modernization and development. This perspective emphasizes the positive contributions of British rule, particularly in terms of economic integration and institutional development.

In contrast, scholars like Edward Said and Shashi Tharoor have critiqued the imperial project for its inherent violence, exploitation, and racism. They argue that the benefits of British rule were unevenly distributed and came at a significant cost to colonized peoples. These historians focus on

the disruptions caused by colonial policies, including the displacement of local industries, the exploitation of labor, and the imposition of foreign cultural norms.

The historiography of the British Empire thus reflects a spectrum of views, ranging from those that highlight its contributions to global development to those that underscore its destructive impacts. This diversity of perspectives underscores the importance of a nuanced understanding of the empire's legacy.

Contributions from sociologists and economists on societal changes

Sociologists and economists have also examined the societal changes wrought by British colonialism, providing insights into how colonial policies shaped social structures, economic systems, and cultural identities.

Sociological studies have examined how colonialism disrupted traditional social structures and established new social hierarchies. The imposition of Western education, legal systems, and cultural norms frequently widened the gap between the colonial elite and the general population. This divide has had lasting impacts on social cohesion and identity, as seen in the ongoing struggles for cultural revival and recognition in many former colonies.

Economists have focused on the economic legacies of British colonialism, particularly the extractive nature of colonial economies. The focus on resource extraction and monoculture agriculture left many former colonies with economies that depended heavily on the export of primary commodities. This economic dependency has hindered efforts to diversify economies and achieve sustainable development.

Economic analyses have also highlighted the ways in which colonial policies created financial dependencies. The reliance on British investment for infrastructure projects and the establishment of trade patterns that favored the metropole created long-term economic imbalances, which have contributed to ongoing challenges in achieving financial self-sufficiency and development.

Comprehensive analysis of how these decisions shape contemporary issues

A comprehensive analysis of the British Empire's legacy reveals how historical, sociological, and economic factors intersect to shape contemporary issues in former colonies. The impacts of colonial policies are evident in various aspects of modern life, from political instability and economic dependency to social inequality and cultural identity.

Political instability in many former colonies can be traced back to the arbitrary borders and governance structures imposed during colonial rule. The lack of experience in self-governance and the artificial divisions created by colonial boundaries have contributed to conflicts and struggles for political stability.

Economic dependency is another significant legacy of British colonialism. The focus on the extraction and export of raw materials created economies that were vulnerable to global market fluctuations. Efforts to diversify and develop local industries have been hampered by the entrenched trade patterns and financial dependencies established during the colonial period.

Colonial legacies also have a significant impact on social inequality and cultural identity. The social hierarchies and class divisions reinforced by colonial policies continue to shape access to education, economic opportunities, and social mobility. Efforts to reclaim and revitalize traditional cultures reflect ongoing struggles to address the cultural disruptions caused by colonial rule.

Overall, the effects of British colonialism are intricate and encompass various aspects. Understanding these legacies requires an interdisciplinary approach that integrates historical, sociological, and economic analyses. By examining the intersections of these factors, we can enhance our understanding of how colonial policies continue to shape contemporary issues in former colonies.

CHAPTER 20

COMPARATIVE COLONIALISM AND GLOBAL IMPACTS

Comparative analyses of British colonial policies with those of other European empires reveal both similarities and differences in their approaches to colonization and their long-term impacts on the colonized regions.

The French Empire, for example, pursued a policy of assimilation, aiming to integrate colonies into a greater French nation. This approach sought to impose French culture, language, and legal systems on the colonized populations, often with little regard for existing local traditions and structures. While this policy created a strong cultural influence, it also led to significant resistance and conflicts, particularly in North Africa.

The Dutch Empire, particularly in Indonesia, focused on economic exploitation and control through trade monopolies and plantation economies. The Dutch East India Company was pivotal in shaping administration and economic policies, creating a highly extractive system that prioritized Dutch interests. This strategy resulted in a legacy of dependency and social stratification in Indonesia.

The Spanish empire's policies were characterized by a combination of religious conversion, economic exploitation, and administrative control. The encomienda system in Latin America exploited Indigenous labor for agricultural and mining activities, leading to significant demographic and social changes. The legacy of Spanish colonialism is evident in the current social and economic inequalities across many Latin American countries.

The Portuguese empire's approach integrated elements of trade, religious conversion, and military conquest. In Brazil and parts of Africa, the Portuguese established plantation economies reliant on slave labor, creating lasting social and economic disparities. The cultural influence of Portuguese rule is also significant, particularly in terms of language and religion.

While the British Empire shared many commonalities with other European empires, such as economic exploitation and cultural imposition, its approach to indirect rule and legal systems was distinctive. The British reliance on existing local power structures, coupled with the establishment of standardized legal systems, had distinct effects on the governance and legal frameworks of former colonies.

Lessons learned and differing impacts

The comparative analysis of different colonial empires highlights several lessons and differing impacts:

1. **Economic exploitation.** All colonial empires engaged in the exploitation of resources and labor, creating economies that depended heavily on the export of primary commodities. This legacy of economic dependency remains a significant challenge for former colonies.

2. **Cultural imposition.** The imposition of European cultures, languages, and religions disrupted local traditions and identities. Efforts to reclaim and revitalize these cultures continue to shape postcolonial societies.

3. **Governance structure.** The administrative and governance structures established by colonial powers influenced the political stability and capacity for self-governance in former colonies. The British approach to indirect rule, while cost-effective, often entrenched traditional hierarchies and created challenges for modern state-building.

4. **Legal systems.** The transplantation of European legal systems had long-term impacts on justice and governance in the former colonies. The British common law system, in particular, created a legal framework that continues to influence contemporary legal practices.

5.   **Social inequality.** Colonial policies reinforced social hierarchies and created significant disparities based on race, ethnicity, and class. Addressing these inequalities is a central concern for postcolonial development.

The lasting effects of British colonial policies can be attributed to several factors:

1. **Institutional legacy.** The British established robust institutions, including legal systems, educational frameworks, and bureaucratic administrations, which continued to function after independence. These institutions provided a foundation for governance but also perpetuated colonial-era inequalities and dependencies.

2. **Economic integration.** Colonial assimilation into global trade and investment networks created deep-rooted economic interdependencies. The resultant export-driven economies left former colonies vulnerable to world market fluctuations and hindered local industrial diversification efforts.

3.   **Cultural influence.** The widespread adoption of the English language and British cultural practices created a lasting cultural influence. This influence enhanced global communication and trade while also contributing to the erosion of Indigenous cultures and identities.

4. **Geopolitical strategies.** British colonial policies were frequently motivated by strategic interests, including the protection of trade routes and the pursuit of global dominance. These strategies influenced the geopolitical landscape and left ongoing conflicts and territorial disputes.

5. **Education and legal systems.** The emphasis on Western education and the establishment of common law legal systems created a lasting legacy that continues to shape educational and legal practices in former colonies. While these systems provided a framework for modernization, they also sidelined the knowledge and legal systems of native populations.

In conclusion, both comparative and global perspectives on colonialism underscore the distinctive and continuous effects of British colonial policies. The institutional, economic, cultural, and geopolitical legacies of British rule persistently shape contemporary issues in former colonies. Understanding these legacies is essential for addressing the ongoing challenges and opportunities for development in the postcolonial world.

Part IX

Environmental Impacts

CHAPTER 21

ENVIRONMENTAL DEGRADATION

Impact of British agricultural policies and resource extraction

The environmental degradation caused by British colonial policies represents an important yet often neglected part of the Empire's legacy. The British approach to agriculture and resource extraction prioritized maximizing economic returns, often at the expense of sustainable environmental practices.

In India, the introduction of cash crops such as indigo, cotton, and tea significantly altered traditional agricultural practices. The focus on monoculture agriculture led to soil depletion, reduced biodiversity, and increased vulnerability to pests and diseases. The British emphasis on large-scale irrigation projects, while boosting agricultural production, also contributed to salinization and waterlogging, further degrading the land.

In Africa, British colonial policies prioritized the extraction of minerals and other resources. The establishment of mines for gold, diamonds, and other precious metals in countries like South Africa, Zimbabwe, and Ghana led to significant

environmental damage. Mining activities caused deforestation, soil erosion, and pollution of water sources, with long-term consequences for local ecosystems and communities.

The exploitation of forests for timber and other resources also has a substantial effect on the environment. In regions such as Southeast Asia and the Caribbean, extensive logging operations led to deforestation and severe loss of biodiversity. The introduction of plantation agriculture, particularly for sugar, rubber, and palm oil, further exacerbated environmental degradation, replacing diverse ecosystems with monoculture plantations.

Long-term environmental consequences in former colonies

Many former colonies have suffered the long-term environmental consequences of British colonial policies. The continued degradation of land and water resources, loss of biodiversity, and disruption of traditional agricultural practices continue to affect these regions.

In India, the legacy of British agricultural policies is seen in the ongoing challenges of soil degradation, water scarcity, and declining agricultural productivity. Efforts to promote sustainable agriculture and restore degraded lands are impeded by entrenched practices and infrastructure established during the colonial period.

In Africa, the environmental damage caused by mining and deforestation has had enduring effects on local communities and ecosystems. The pollution of rivers and groundwater sources from mining activities has compromised access to clean water, negatively altering the health and livelihoods of local populations. Additionally, deforestation has diminished biodiversity and disrupted ecological balance, further contributing to climate change and environmental instability.

The Caribbean islands, heavily impacted by plantation agriculture, face ongoing challenges related to soil erosion, loss of arable land, and vulnerability to natural disasters. The environmental degradation has also altered the tourism industry, a significant source of income for many Caribbean nations.

Case studies: deforestation in India, mining in Africa

Deforestation in India. British colonial policies in India promoted extensive deforestation to meet the demand for timber and to clear land for agriculture. The establishment of railways and the expansion of tea and coffee plantations led to the large-scale clearing of forests. The Forest Act of 1878 further facilitated deforestation by allowing the colonial government to control and exploit forest resources. The long-term consequences of these policies are seen in the loss of forest cover, reduced biodiversity, and environmental degradation.

Mining in Africa. The British exploitation of mineral resources in Africa had severe environmental impacts. In South Africa, gold and diamond mining led to significant land degradation, water pollution, and health hazards for mine workers and nearby communities. The extraction of minerals in Ghana, particularly gold, caused deforestation, soil erosion, and contamination of water bodies with toxic chemicals. These environmental issues continue to affect the health and livelihoods of local populations and pose challenges for sustainable development.

Part X

Social and Human Rights Issues

CHAPTER 22

LABOR AND TRADE PRACTICES

British colonial labor policies were characterized by the exploitation and coercion of local populations to serve colonial economic interests. These measures included the use of forced labor, indentured servitude, and oppressive working conditions.

The transatlantic slave trade is one of the most egregious examples of British labor exploitation. Countless Africans were forcibly transported under duress to the Americas and subjected to brutal conditions on plantations. The legacy of slavery has left deep social and economic scars in the Caribbean, the Americas, and Africa, contributing to ongoing racial inequalities and social injustices.

Following the abolition of slavery, the British introduced the system of indentured servitude to meet labor demands in colonies such as the Caribbean, Fiji, and Southeast Asia. Workers, primarily from India and China, were recruited under contracts that promised wages and an eventual return to their homeland. However, these laborers often faced harsh conditions, inadequate pay, and limited freedom, effectively replacing one form of coerced labor with another.

In Africa, the British employed forced labor for infrastructure projects and resource extraction. Indigenous people were compelled to work on roads, railways, and mines, typically under brutal conditions. These labor policies disrupted traditional livelihoods and contributed to social and economic dislocation.

Impact on social structures and demographics

British labor and trade practices had serious effects on social structures and demographics in the colonies. The forced migration and exploitation of labor led to the formation of multiethnic and multiracial societies, but also entrenched social hierarchies and economic disparities.

In the Caribbean, the legacy of slavery and indentured servitude resulted in a complex social structure characterized by racial and ethnic divisions. The descendants of enslaved Africans, indentured laborers, and European settlers formed distinct social groups with varying degrees of economic power and social status. These divisions have shaped social relations, identity politics, and economic opportunities in the region.

In India, the recruitment of indentured labor for overseas work resulted in the formation of Indian diaspora communities in regions such as Mauritius, Trinidad, Fiji, and Malaysia. Although these communities have enriched the cultural and economic diversity of their host countries, they have also encountered challenges related to social integration, discrimination, and financial exploitation.

In Africa, colonial labor policies disrupted traditional social structures and economic systems. Forced labor and the introduction of cash economies eroded communal land ownership and subsistence farming, leading to social dislocation and heightened dependence on wage labor. The legacy of these policies continues to influence social and economic dynamics in many African countries.

Long-term economic and social implications

The long-term economic and social implications of British labor and trade practices are significant and continue to shape former colonies.

Economically, the legacy of exploitation has contributed to persistent poverty, inequality, and underdevelopment. The extraction of wealth and resources for the benefit of the colonial powers left many colonies with weak economic foundations and limited capacity for self-sustained growth. The disruption of traditional economies and the creation of monoculture economies have made former colonies vulnerable to global market fluctuations and economic instability.

Socially, the legacy of British labor policies has contributed to social hierarchies and divisions. The exploitation of labor and the imposition of social hierarchies based on race and ethnicity have created deep-seated inequalities and social tensions. Efforts to address these legacies and promote social justice and equity are ongoing, but the entrenched nature of these issues poses significant challenges.

In conclusion, British labor and trade practices during the colonial period markedly and permanently altered social structures, demographics, and economic development in former colonies. The exploitation of labor, forced migrations, and the creation of monoculture economies have left a legacy of inequality and underdevelopment. Addressing these legacies requires comprehensive efforts to promote economic diversification, social inclusion, and historical justice. Understanding the full extent of these impacts is essential for fostering fair development and reconciliation in the postcolonial world.

EPILOGUE

As we draw the narrative of the British Empire to a close, it is essential to reflect on the broad spectrum of legacies it has left behind. The British Empire was an unprecedented force in world history, shaping the geopolitical, economic, social, and cultural landscapes of vast swathes of the globe. Its reach was both expansive and powerful, influencing countries and regions in ways that remain evident today.

One of the most significant legacies of the British Empire is the global proliferation of the English language and British cultural norms. English has become the global lingua franca, facilitating international communication, trade, and diplomacy. British cultural influences, from legal systems to educational frameworks, continue to permeate many former colonies, shaping their contemporary identities and institutional structures.

However, these legacies come with a complex and often painful history of exploitation, displacement, and cultural imposition. The economic structures established during the colonial period created deep-seated dependencies and inequalities that many former colonies continue to grapple with. The forced movement of people through slavery and indentured labor has left indelible marks on the social fabric of numerous societies, contributing to persistent struggles with racial and ethnic divisions.

The environmental impact of British colonial policies, characterized by resource extraction and the introduction of non-native species, has had lasting consequences for the ecosystems of many regions. The historical context of these environmental changes exacerbates the problems of deforestation, soil degradation, and biodiversity loss, necessitating comprehensive and context-sensitive approaches to conservation and sustainability.

The legal and administrative frameworks established by the British Empire have also left a mixed legacy. While the introduction of common law systems provided a basis for legal order and governance, the imposition of these systems often conflicted with local traditions and practices, leading to enduring tensions and challenges in achieving legal coherence and justice.

Lessons for the future

Understanding the complex legacies of the British Empire is not merely an academic endeavor; it provides vital lessons for contemporary global challenges. The history of the Empire illustrates the importance of confronting historical injustices and promoting reconciliation. This means acknowledging the lasting effects of colonial policies on current social, economic, and political dynamics and actively working to address these legacies.

One of the key lessons is the need for inclusive and participatory approaches to governance and development. The imposition of colonial rule often excluded local populations from decision-making processes, leading to policies that did not reflect their needs or aspirations. In the postcolonial context, promoting inclusive governance that empowers marginalized communities and respects local knowledge and traditions is essential for sustainable development and social cohesion.

Economic diversification and self-sufficiency are also fundamental lessons from the colonial experience. The dependency on monoculture economies and the extraction of raw materials left many former colonies vulnerable to global market fluctuations. Building resilient and diversified economies that prioritize local industries and sustainable practices is imperative for long-term development.

Environmental sustainability is another vital lesson. The degradation caused by colonial exploitation emphasizes the importance of adopting sustainable and ecologically sensitive approaches to development. Efforts to restore and protect ecosystems must be integrated with broader socio-economic policies to ensure that conservation benefits both nature and local communities.

Finally, the importance of cultural revival and recognition cannot be overstated. The suppression of Indigenous cultures and identities during the colonial period has had profound and lasting effects. Supporting cultural revival and ensuring the recognition and respect of diverse cultural traditions are essential for fostering a sense of identity and belonging, which are crucial for social stability and harmony.

To conclude, the legacy of the British Empire is a complex framework shaped by both progress and exploitation. Reflecting on this history provides invaluable insights into the challenges and opportunities we face today and in the future. By learning from the past, we can work toward building a more just, more inclusive, and sustainable world where the echoes of colonialism are met with a commitment to reconciliation and equity.

Additional key themes and perspectives

Although the catastrophic decisions and their immediate consequences have been thoroughly examined, several other key themes and perspectives also need to be addressed to fully understand the British Empire's legacy.

Economic exploitation and global trade networks

The economic exploitation of colonies was a central aspect of British imperialism. This exploitation involved the extraction of raw materials, the establishment of plantation economies, and the creation of trade networks that mainly benefited the British metropole. The colonial economic policies frequently left colonies dependent on a limited selection of exports, making them vulnerable to global market fluctuations. Consequently, these policies have led to ongoing economic underdevelopment and inequality.

Primary consequences:

- Economic dependency and lack of diversification.
- Vulnerability to global market changes.
- Entrenched economic inequalities.

Cultural suppression and Revival

The British Empire's cultural policies aimed to suppress and assimilate local traditions and practices. This included the imposition of English as the medium of education and administration, the suppression of Indigenous languages and customs, and the promotion of Western cultural norms. The long-term impact of these policies has been the erosion of cultural identities and the ongoing struggle for cultural revival and recognition.

Primary consequences:

- Loss of Indigenous languages and traditions.
- Cultural alienation and identity crises.
- Movements for cultural revival and decolonization of education.

Environmental degradation

The environmental impact of British colonial policies was profound. The focus on resource extraction and the introduction of non-native species led to significant ecological damage. Deforestation, soil depletion, and biodiversity loss are some of the long-lasting environmental consequences that former colonies continue to grapple with.

Primary consequences:

- Environmental degradation and loss of biodiversity.
- Long-term challenges in sustainable development.
- Need for extensive ecological restoration efforts.

Human rights and social justice

The British Empire's legacy includes numerous human rights abuses, such as the brutal suppression of uprisings, forced labor, and exploitation. These actions have left deep scars and have necessitated ongoing efforts for justice and reconciliation. The crucial step toward healing and fair societies is addressing historical injustices.

Primary consequences:

- Intergenerational trauma and social unrest.
- Ongoing demands for reparations and justice.
- Efforts to document and acknowledge historical atrocities.

Political fragmentation and instability

The political structures imposed by the British, including the use of indirect rule and the arbitrary drawing of borders, have led to lasting political fragmentation and instability. Many former colonies have struggled with internal conflicts, weak governance, and challenges in building cohesive nation-states.

Primary consequences:

- Persistent ethnic and regional conflicts.
- Challenges in establishing stable governance.
- Efforts to create inclusive political frameworks.

Addressing the legacies of the British Empire requires a multifaceted approach that includes:

1. **Reconciliation and justice.** Acknowledging historical injustices, providing reparations, and fostering reconciliation processes.

2. **Economic diversification and development.** Promoting economic policies that reduce dependency on single exports and encourage sustainable development.

3. **Cultural revitalization.** Supporting initiatives that revive and protect Indigenous cultures, languages, and traditions.

4. **Environmental restoration.** Implementing policies and projects that restore degraded ecosystems and promote sustainable environmental practices.

5. **Inclusive governance.** Building political systems that are inclusive and reflective of the diverse populations within former colonies.

The British Empire's catastrophic decisions have left a lasting imprint that continues to shape the modern world. The effects of colonialism are far-reaching and diverse, including economic dependency, cultural suppression, environmental degradation, and human rights abuses. By understanding and confronting these consequences, we can work toward a more just, equitable, and sustainable future. Reconciliation, justice, and respect for the rights of all those affected by colonial rule are necessary commitments. Only through such comprehensive efforts can we hope to move beyond the shadows of colonialism and build a world that respects the dignity and diversity of its inhabitants.

Appendix A
Key Figures

Sir Mark Sykes (1879–1919)

Sir Mark Sykes was a British diplomat and politician known for his role in the Sykes-Picot Agreement of 1916, which secretly divided the Ottoman Empire's territories in the Middle East between Britain and France. Born into a wealthy family, Sykes was educated at Jesus College, Cambridge, and developed a keen interest in the Middle East. As a diplomat, he traveled extensively in the region and became an expert on its affairs. His work laid the foundations for modern Middle Eastern geopolitics, but the arbitrary borders drawn under his guidance have contributed to conflicts and instability.

François Georges-Picot (1870–1951)

François Georges-Picot was a French diplomat who co-negotiated the Sykes-Picot Agreement with Sir Mark Sykes. Born into a prominent legal family, Picot entered the French diplomatic service and specialized in Middle Eastern affairs. The agreement he co-authored with Sykes aimed to delineate spheres of influence in the Middle East between France and Britain, setting the stage for future tensions and divisions in the region. Picot's work has had lasting implications, influencing the political boundaries and conflicts in the Middle East to this day.

Arthur Balfour (1848–1930)

Arthur Balfour was a British Conservative politician who acted as Prime Minister from 1902 to 1905 and later as foreign secretary. He is best known for the Balfour Declaration of 1917, which expressed British commitment to the formation of a "national home for the Jewish people" in Palestine. This declaration was a pivotal moment in the history of the Middle East, significantly impacting Jewish-Arab relations and contributing to the ongoing Israeli-Palestinian conflict. Balfour's legacy is a subject of intense debate, reflecting the complexities of British imperial policies.

Sir Cyril Radcliffe (1899–1977)

Sir Cyril Radcliffe was a British lawyer and judge who was tasked with drawing the borders between India and Pakistan in 1947, a process that became known as the Radcliffe Line. With no prior experience in India, Radcliffe was given just five weeks to complete his task. The hurried and arbitrary nature of his border demarcation led to widespread violence, displacement, and enduring conflicts, particularly in the Kashmir region. Radcliffe's work remains a controversial and tragic chapter in the history of the Indian subcontinent.

Lord Louis Mountbatten (1900–1979)

Lord Louis Mountbatten was the final viceroy of India and the inaugural governor-general of independent India. Appointed viceroy in 1947, he oversaw the final stages of British rule and the partition of India and Pakistan. Mountbatten's decisions during this critical period have been both praised and criticized. While he played a key role in facilitating a rapid transition to independence, his handling of the partition process contributed to the violence and chaos that ensued. Mountbatten's legacy is intertwined with the complex and often painful history of Indian independence.

Jomo Kenyatta (1897–1978)

Jomo Kenyatta was a Kenyan anti-colonial activist and politician who became the first president of Kenya. A key figure in the struggle for independence from British rule, Kenyatta was imprisoned during the Mau Mau Uprising. After his release, he led Kenya to independence in 1963 and served as president until he died in 1978. Kenyatta's leadership helped shape modern Kenya, but his tenure also faced criticism for its authoritarian tendencies. His role in the fight against colonialism and his impact on Kenya's post-independence trajectory are central to his legacy.

Kwame Nkrumah (1909–1972)

Kwame Nkrumah was a Ghanaian nationalist leader who was instrumental in the country's independence movement and became its first prime minister and president. Educated in the United States and the United Kingdom, Nkrumah returned to Ghana to lead the Convention People's Party (CPP) and spearhead the struggle against British colonial rule. Ghana's independence in 1957 marked a significant milestone in African decolonization. Nkrumah's vision of Pan-Africanism and his efforts to promote African unity have left a lasting legacy despite political challenges during his presidency.

Mahatma Gandhi (1869–1948)

Mahatma Gandhi, an Indian lawyer, political ethicist, and anti-colonial nationalist who led India's struggle for independence from British rule. Renowned for his philosophy of nonviolent resistance, or Satyagraha, Gandhi mobilized millions through campaigns including the Quit India Movement and the Salt March. His leadership and vision were instrumental in achieving Indian independence in 1947. Gandhi's commitment to nonviolence and social justice has inspired movements worldwide, making him a global icon of peace and human rights.

Jawaharlal Nehru (1889–1964)

Jawaharlal Nehru, a prominent Indian nationalist leader and the first Prime Minister of independent India. A staunch ally of Mahatma Gandhi, Nehru was a key architect of the Indian independence movement and the shaping of modern India. As Prime Minister, he implemented policies aimed at economic modernization, social reform, and secularism. Nehru's legacy includes his contributions to India's democratic institutions, his vision for a pluralistic society, and the challenges and controversies associated with his leadership.

Subhas Chandra Bose (1897–1945)

An Indian nationalist leader, Subhas Chandra Bose, championed armed resistance against British rule. Dissatisfied with the nonviolent approach of Gandhi and the Indian National Congress, Bose formed the Indian National Army (INA) with Japanese support during World War II. His efforts to secure India's independence through military means have made him a controversial yet revered figure in Indian history. Bose's unwavering dedication to India's freedom and his unconventional strategy for achieving it will live on in his legacy.

General Reginald Dyer (1864–1927)

General Reginald Dyer was a British Army officer best known for his role in the Amritsar Massacre of 1919. With callous disregard for human life, Dyer ordered his soldiers to indiscriminately shoot into a crowd of innocent, unarmed civilians congregated peacefully at Jallianwala Bagh, resulting in hundreds of deaths. This brutal act shocked the world and galvanized the Indian independence movement. Dyer's actions have been widely condemned as a symbol of colonial oppression and brutality, highlighting the darker aspects of British rule in India.

Lord Frederick Lugard (1858–1945)

Lord Frederick Lugard was a British colonial administrator and the architect of the policy of indirect rule in Africa. With experience in governmental roles across Uganda, Nigeria, and Hong Kong, Lugard advocated for governing through existing local power structures rather than imposing direct British control. His dual-mandate policy aimed to promote economic development while maintaining social order. Lugard's approach to colonial administration shaped British policy throughout the empire while also reinforcing traditional hierarchies and contributing to political fragmentation in postcolonial Africa.

Lord Curzon (1859–1925)

Lord George Nathaniel Curzon, a leading British politician, assumed the role of Viceroy of India from 1899 to 1905. His tenure featured significant administrative reforms, including the reorganization of the Indian army, police, and civil services. While Curzon's policies aimed to enhance British control and efficiency, they also faced criticism for their paternalistic and autocratic nature. The partition of Bengal in 1905, intended to improve administrative efficiency, provoked strong opposition, and was eventually reversed. Curzon's legacy in India is a complex one, reflecting both his contributions to governance and the controversies surrounding his policies.

Appendix B
Timeline of Key Events

1600s

1600: Formation of the East India Company

Queen Elizabeth I granted the East India Company a royal charter, marking the beginning of British commercial interest in India and the wider Asian region.

1700s

1757: Battle of Plassey

British forces, led by Robert Clive, defeated the Nawab of Bengal, establishing British control over Bengal and laying the foundation for British dominance in India.

1763: Treaty of Paris

The treaty ends the Seven Years' War, with France ceding significant territories in North America to Britain, including Canada, marking a significant expansion of the British Empire.

1800s

1833: Abolition of Slavery Act

The British Parliament passes the Abolition of Slavery Act, ending slavery in the British Empire and emancipating enslaved people in the Caribbean, Africa, and other colonies.

1839–1842: First Opium War

Britain waged war against China to force the Qing Dynasty to allow the importation of opium, leading to the Treaty of Nanking and the cession of Hong Kong to Britain.

1857–1858: Indian Rebellion

This massive rebellion against British rule in India resulted in the dismantling of the East India Company, paving the way for direct British governance under the Raj.

1884–1885: Berlin Conference

European powers, including Britain, convened to divide Africa into spheres of influence, initiating the "Scramble for Africa" and leading to the arbitrary drawing of borders.

1900s

1916: Sykes-Picot Agreement

In a clandestine agreement, Britain and France conspired to divide the Ottoman Empire's Middle Eastern territories, imposing artificial borders that have fueled regional instability for generations.

1917: Balfour Declaration

Britain issues the Balfour Declaration, expressing support for the establishment of a national home for the Jewish people in Palestine, impacting Jewish-Arab relations.

1919: Amritsar Massacre

British troops, under General Dyer, massacred hundreds of unarmed Indian civilians gathered in Jallianwala Bagh, Amritsar, galvanizing the Indian independence movement.

1947: Partition of India

British India is partitioned into two independent dominions, India and Pakistan, leading to massive population displacement, communal violence, and the Kashmir conflict.

1952–1960: Mau Mau Uprising

The Kikuyu people of Kenya rebel against British colonial rule. The British suppressed the uprising with brutal measures, including detention camps and widespread human rights abuses.

1956: Suez Crisis

Britain, along with France and Israel, invaded Egypt after President Nasser's decision to nationalize the Suez Canal. International pressure forced a withdrawal, marking a decline in British influence.

1960: Nigerian Independence

Nigeria gained independence from Britain, transitioning from colonial rule to self-governance but facing challenges related to ethnic divisions and political instability.

1963: Kenyan Independence

Kenya achieves independence from Britain, marking the end of the Mau Mau Uprising era and the beginning of a new phase of self-governance under Jomo Kenyatta.

1965: Rhodesian Unilateral Declaration of Independence

Rhodesia (modern-day Zimbabwe) declared independence unilaterally under a white-minority government, leading to international isolation and conflict until majority rule was established in 1980.

1997: Handover of Hong Kong

Britain returned Hong Kong to China under the principle of "one country, two systems," ending 156 years of British colonial rule and significantly impacting Hong Kong's future.

2000s

2013: British Government Apology for Mau Mau Abuses

The British government released a formal apology and agreed to compensate thousands of Kenyans tortured and abused during the Mau Mau Uprising, acknowledging the atrocities committed during colonial rule.

Appendix C

Amritsar Massacre

A tragic event occurred in 1919 when British troops under General Reginald Dyer fired on a peaceful gathering in Jallianwala Bagh, Amritsar, India, resulting in hundreds of civilian deaths. This massacre galvanized the Indian independence movement and highlighted the brutality of British colonial rule.

Balfour Declaration

In 1917, Arthur Balfour, British Foreign Secretary, released a statement expressing the British government's support for establishing a "national home for the Jewish people" in Palestine. This declaration had a significant impact on Jewish-Arab relations and altered the geopolitical terrain of the Middle East.

Berlin Conference

A meeting held in Berlin in 1884–1885 saw European powers, including Britain, divide Africa into spheres of influence without consideration for existing ethnic or political boundaries. This conference initiated the "Scramble for Africa" and led to arbitrary borders that have contributed to long-term conflicts in the region.

British East India Company

A British trading company established in 1600 was a primary catalyst for the growth of British power in India and other parts of Asia. The company's policies and actions led to significant economic exploitation and political control, eventually resulting in direct British rule in India.

Colonization

The process by which a country establishes control over a foreign territory often involves the exploitation of resources, imposition of cultural norms, and displacement of local populations. The British Empire's extensive colonization significantly altered the social, economic, and political landscapes of the regions it occupied.

Commonwealth of Nations

An intergovernmental organization of countries, most of which were former territories of the British Empire. The Commonwealth promotes economic cooperation, political stability, and cultural exchange among its member states.

Cultural Assimilation

The transformation of a minority group or culture comes from conforming to the customs, language, and social behaviors of the dominant culture. During the British Empire, policies aimed at cultural assimilation frequently led to the suppression of Indigenous cultures and traditions.

Decolonization

The process by which colonies gain independence from colonial powers. Political movements, negotiations, and occasionally conflicts characterized this process, which resulted in the establishment of sovereign states. The mid-20th century saw a significant wave of decolonization, particularly in Africa and Asia.

Indentured Servitude

Indentured servitude was a system of labor in which individuals were contracted to work for a specified period in exchange for passage to a new country as well as room and board. After the abolition of slavery, the British employed this system to fulfill labor demands in colonies like the Caribbean, Southeast Asia, and Africa.

Indirect Rule

A colonial policy of governing through existing local power structures and traditional leaders rather than direct administration by colonial officials. This approach was widely used by the British in Africa and Asia to maintain control while minimizing administrative costs.

Indian National Congress (INC)

A political organization established in India in 1885 that was instrumental in the nation's liberation from British colonial rule. Mahatma Gandhi and Jawaharlal Nehru were regarded as some of the preeminent leaders who rose to prominence within the INC and subsequently defined the trajectory of independent India.

Mau Mau Uprising

An insurrection against British colonial authority in Kenya, led by the Kikuyu people from 1952 to 1960. The British response involved widespread detentions, torture, and human rights abuses. This uprising played a significant role in Kenya's journey to independence.

Monoculture

The agricultural practice of repeatedly planting the same crop across a large expanse of land for many consecutive years. During the British Empire, colonies were often converted into monoculture economies focused on cash crops like cotton, tea, and rubber, leading to ecological and economic vulnerabilities.

Partition of India

The split of British India into two independent dominions, India and Pakistan, took place in 1947. The partition resulted in massive population displacement, communal violence, and the ongoing Kashmir conflict.

Protectorate

A state or territory controlled and protected by another. In the context of the British Empire, protectorates were regions where local rulers retained some degree of sovereignty under British oversight, such as the Trucial States (modern-day United Arab Emirates).

Raj

This term describes British rule in India from 1858 to 1947, following the end of East India Company control. The British Raj was characterized by significant economic, social, and political changes in India.

Satyagraha

Satyagraha is a philosophy and strategy of nonviolent resistance developed by Mahatma Gandhi during the Indian independence movement. It emphasizes the power of truth and moral force in political struggle.

Scramble for Africa

A period during the late nineteenth century when European powers rapidly colonized and divided Africa. The Berlin Conference formalized this scramble, leading to the arbitrary drawing of borders and significant long-term impacts on African nations.

Sykes-Picot Agreement

The Sykes-Picot Agreement was a secret 1916 accord between Britain and France, with Russia's assent, to divide the Ottoman Empire's territories in the Middle East into spheres of influence. This agreement laid the groundwork for modern Middle Eastern boundaries and ongoing conflicts.

Transatlantic Slave Trade

The forced mass exodus of Africans to the Americas, perpetrated by European colonial powers such as Britain, characterized the transatlantic slave trade from the sixteenth to the nineteenth centuries. This trade resulted in the exploitation and suffering of millions and had lasting social and economic impacts on both Africa and the Americas.

The Treaty of Nanking, ratified in 1842, brought an end to the First Opium War between Britain and China. This treaty marked a turning point in the consolidation of British hegemony over China, granting Britain sovereignty over Hong Kong and access to key Chinese ports.

References and Further Reading

Books and articles:

Anderson, David M. Histories of the Hanged: The Dirty War in Kenya and the End of Empire. W. W. Norton & Company, 2005.

Bayly, C. A. The Birth of the Modern World, 1780–1914: Global Connections and Comparisons. Blackwell Publishing, 2004.

Brown, Judith M. Gandhi: Prisoner of Hope. Yale University Press, 1991.

Cannadine, David. Ornamentalism: How the British Saw Their Empire. Oxford University Press, 2001.

Darwin, John. The Empire Project: The Rise and Fall of the British World-System, 1830–1970. Cambridge University Press, 2009.

Ferguson, Niall. Empire: The Rise and Demise of the British World Order and the Lessons for Global Power. Basic Books, 2003.

Fryer, Peter. Staying Power: The History of Black People in Britain. Pluto Press, 1984.

Hyam, Ronald. Britain's Declining Empire: The Road to Decolonisation, 1918–1968. Cambridge University Press, 2007.

Judd, Denis. The Lion and the Tiger: The Rise and Fall of the British Raj, 1600–1947. Oxford University Press, 2004.

Metcalf, Thomas R., and Barbara D. Metcalf. A Concise History of India. Cambridge University Press, 2001.

Nkrumah, Kwame. Africa Must Unite. Panaf Books, 1963.

Pakenham, Thomas. The Scramble for Africa: White Man's Conquest of the Dark Continent from 1876 to 1912. Avon Books, 1991.

Said, Edward. Culture and Imperialism. Knopf, 1994.

Tharoor, Shashi. Inglorious Empire: What the British Did to India. Hurst Publishers, 2017.

Primary sources and historical documents:

"The Sykes-Picot Agreement" (1916). Available at the National Archives.

"The Balfour Declaration" (1917). Available at the National Archives.

"The Indian Independence Act" (1947). Available at the UK Parliament Archives.

"The Treaty of Nanking" (1842). Available at the British Library.

"The Government of India Act" (1935). Available at the National Archives of India.

Reports and official records:

"The Radcliffe Boundary Commission Report." (1947). Available at the National Archives of India.

"Report of the Amritsar Massacre Commission." (1920). Available at the National Archives

Journals and academic papers:

Chakrabarty, Dipesh. Postcoloniality and the Artifice of History: Who Speaks for 'Indian' Pasts?" Representations, vol. 37, 1992, pp. 1–26.

Mamdani, Mahmood. Citizen and Subject: Contemporary Africa and the Legacy of Late Colonialism. Princeton University Press, 1996.

Metcalf, Barbara D. Islam and Power in Colonial India: The Making and Unmaking of a Muslim 'Community.' Comparative Studies in Society and History, vol. 31, no. 2, 1989, pp. 211-223.

Ranger, Terence. The Invention of Tradition in Colonial Africa. African Affairs, vol. 82, no. 328, 1983, pp. 234–248.

Online resources:

"The British empire." The British empire Online (www.britishempire.co.uk](http://www.britishempire.co.uk/).

"The National Archives: Colonial History." The National Archives, UK (www.nationalarchives.gov.uk](http://www.nationalarchives.gov.uk/).

"Gandhi Heritage Portal." GandhiServe Foundation (www.gandhiheritageportal.org](http://www.gandhiheritageportal.org/)

"British Library: India Office Records." British Library (www.bl.uk/collection-guides/india-office-records).